A SINGULAR BEAUTY

A Memoir

By

JEROME CHARYN

ISBN: 978-0-578-82531-1

ASIN: B08MZC6HFP

STAY THIRSTY PRESS

An Imprint of Stay Thirsty Publishing

A Division of

STAY THIRSTY MEDIA, INC.

staythirstypublishing.com

Recent Books by Jerome Charyn

The Secret Life of Emily Dickinson

Johnny One Eye: A Tale of the American Revolution

I Am Abraham: A Novel of Lincoln and the Civil War

CESARE: A Novel of War-Torn Berlin

Sergeant Salinger

A
SINGULAR
BEAUTY

A Memoir

By

JEROME CHARYN

For Faigele and Sergeant Sam

Letter from Mogilev

We would walk the streets, a prodigy in short pants and his mother, so defiantly beautiful that all transactions stopped, and we'd enter a slow-motion world where women, men, children, dogs, cats, and firemen in their trucks would look at her with such longing in their eyes, that I felt like some usurper who was carrying her off to another hill. I was only five in '42, a nervous boy who couldn't spell his own name. My mother wore her silver fox coat, designed and cut for her by my father, Sam, who was a foreman in a Manhattan fur shop. The coat was contraband, and should have gone to the Navy. My father's shop had a contract with the War Department to supply the Navy with fur-lined vests so its admirals and ordinary sailors wouldn't freeze to death aboard some battleship.

It was a darkly romantic time. The Bronx sat near the Atlantic Ocean without a proper seawall, and there was talk of attack squads arriving in little rubber boats off some tricky submarine, getting into the sewer system, and gobbling up my native ground. But I never saw a Nazi on our walks. And what power would any of them have had against the shimmering outline of my mother in her silver fox coat? She was born in 1911, like Ginger Rogers and Jean Harlow, but she didn't have their platinum look: she was the dark lady from Belorusse.

We weren't on a pleasure stroll. It was our daily trip to the post office, where my mother was expecting a letter from Mogilev, in White Russia, where her brother lived, a school-teacher who'd raised her after their own mother had died. I'm not sure why this letter couldn't have been delivered to the mailbox in our building. Had the Germans seized Mogilev, and my uncle could only write via some secret system in the Soviet underground?

The postmaster would always come out from behind his window when my mother appeared. He was a cranky little man who wore slippers and liked to shout at his clerks. But he was kind to the dark lady's little boy. He would take me through his side of the wall and show me the "graveyard," a gigantic sack where all the dead letters lay, sad undeliverable things, with postmarks from all over the planet. I would sift through the pile, look at the pictures on the stamps, smell the glue, while the postmaster squeezed my mother's hand. But not even this wizard of the mail could produce a letter from Mogilev.

She would tremble on the journey home as we climbed hill after hill. She walked like a drunken lady. It was from my mother that I learned how memory could kill. She could survive as long as she had word from Mogilev. But there was no word in the middle of a war, only mountains of dead-letter boxes between Belorusse and the Bronx.

She started smoking cigarettes. And I had to smother a fallen match and slap at the little fires that seemed to collect in her wake. I would dust the walls with a dry mop and attend to my mother's goose, opening the oven door to stab at the bird with a fork, until it was the way my father liked it, dark and crisp and unchewable.

I would put his whisky on the table, pour him a shot, and jabber endlessly, ask him whatever nonsense came into my head, to camouflage my mother's silences. But as soon as he left the house, she would pretend that her brother was calling from Mogilev (we didn't even have a telephone), and she'd laugh and cry in a Russian that was so melodious, I would get confused until I believed that *all* language was born on a phantom phone.

Her English had no music; it was halting and cruel, like a twisted tongue. But I was a clever little bastard. I would clutch at her phrases like building blocks and sing my own backward sentence-songs. "In the sea, mama, drowns many broken ships."

I'd never been to the sea. But I could imagine the great Atlantic where those German subs prowled like crocodiles. My mother had promised to take me across the bridge into Manhattan and watch the ocean liners that lay hobbled in the Hudson and couldn't get into the war. But there was always that letter from Mogilev on her mind, and she didn't seem able to plot the simple logic of our trip.

And so we were marooned in the Bronx. My mother got more morose. She would stand in front of the mirror for an hour with a pot of rouge and a canister of lipstick and paint her face. Then she'd start to cry and ruin all the work she did, enormous teardrops eating into the paint with their own salty acid. I'd follow her into the street and head for the post office, people staring at this flaw in the dark lady, the tracks in her face. It couldn't have made her less appealing, because the postmaster was twice as attentive.

"Some coffee, Mrs. Charyn?" he said, and coffee was hard to find. He'd have pieces of candy for me, and cups of cocoa, which marked my own lips. But my mother was deeply discouraged. The pain had eaten into her ritual.

"No letter Mogilev?"

"It will come, Mrs. Charyn. Russian letters are notorious. They ride very slow, but they never fail."

He'd dance around her in his slippers, scowl at his clerks, pirouette with his coffeepot, but my mother hardly noticed. She hadn't risked disappointment day after day to become part of his coffee club. He couldn't have charmed her with all the candy in the world.

And I was lost at sea. I had to pilot my mother from place to place, undress her, cook my father's goose. But I was getting lucky. I didn't have to go to school. Kindergarten had been canceled in the Bronx. There was a terrible shortage of teachers, and someone must have figured that five-year-olds like me could sit at home with wooden blocks and a pound of clay. I didn't have time for clay. I had to groom my mother, coax her into shape, fool my father into believing she was perfectly fine. I fed him Scotch and gin. He was wall-eyed when he left the dinner table. He would ask my mother questions, and I would answer, once, twice, until I got slapped.

"Mind your business, Baby."

Baby, that's what he would call his own kid to make him suffer. I couldn't read or write, but I could listen to the radio. I heard the battle reports, how the British commandos were making amphibious landings in the middle of the desert, and knocking the hell out of Hitler's Africa Corps. I asked my father to call me Soldier or Little Sergeant, but he never did.

Dad was the sergeant, not me. Cutting fur-lined vests for a lot of admirals had kept him out of the war, but he still had his own uniform: a white helmet that looked like a shallow pot and a white armband with a complicated insignia (a blue circle with a triangle of red and white stripes sitting inside). My father was an air-raid warden with the rank of sergeant. He would patrol the streets after dark with a silver whistle around his neck and make sure that every single window in his assigned radius of blocks had a blackout curtain. If a light blazed from a window, he'd warn you with his whistle and shout, "Lights out, smarty." And if that didn't work, he could call the cops or summon you before the Civilian Defense Board. He was an impeccable warden, my dad, heartless within his own small hegemony, willing to risk the wrath of friends, neighbors, anyone who misbehaved. He'd herd you into a cellar if he ever caught you in the street during an air-raid drill. Some people wouldn't listen to Sergeant Sam, some rebelled, beat him into the ground until other wardens arrived, or a cop rescued him. Even in '42, his first year as a warden, he had a medal from Mayor LaGuardia, chief of Civilian Defense. I caught LaGuardia on the radio. "We have our soldiers in Brooklyn and the Bronx, brave men who go forth without a gun, who guard the home front against saboteurs and unpatriotic people. What would I do without my wardens?"

And if dad came home with a bruised eye and a broken whistle, his armband torn, a big dent in his white hat, it was the Baby who had to search for Mercurochrome, while my mother sat forlorn in the living room, dreaming of Russian mail. He was much more solicitous in moments of sorrow, almost endearing with dirt on his face. He'd clutch my hand, look at FDR's picture on the wall, while I swabbed his eye with a cotton stick.

"Baby, shouldn't we write to the President?"

"He's busy, dad, he's drowning in mail. A warden can't complain. How would it look if you snitch? You'll give the Bronx a bad name."

Of course I couldn't speak in full flowing sentences. My melody went something like this: "Drownin', dad, the prez. Eatin' vanilla envelopes. And you better be quiet. The Bronx will kill a tattytale."

Dad got my drift.

"Who's a tattytale?"

But he wouldn't have slapped me with Franklin Delano Roosevelt on the wall. Even in her distraction, my mother blessed FDR whenever she lit a candle. The blood that flowed in him was our blood too.

Anyway, dad couldn't have written to Roosevelt. He was as unlettered as I was, as feeble with the pen. He could barely scratch a few words in his Civilian Defense reports. And so he suffered quietly, licked his wounds, and we went to church on the high holidays, with his face still black and blue. I had to dress my mother, make sure her mascara didn't run. We didn't belong to that temple on the Grand Concourse, Adath Israel, with its white stone pillars and big brass door. Adath Israel was where all the millionaire doctors and lawyers went. The services were held in English. The assistant rabbi at Adath Israel was also a painter and a poet. He gave classes at night for kids in the neighborhood. We called him Len. He was in love with the dark lady. That's why he encouraged me, let me into his class. He wanted us to join the temple, but my father wouldn't go near any place that didn't have a cantor. That was the disadvantage of English. A cantor would have had nothing to sing.

We went to the old synagogue at the bottom of the hill. It was made of crumbling brick; portions of the steeple would rain down from the roof. There had been three fires at the synagogue since the war began, and the "incendiary bomb," as we called it, was always about to close. But we had Gilbert Rogovin, who'd been a choirboy here and had studied at the cantors' college in Cincinnati, Ohio. Our cantor could have made a fortune singing holy songs on Fifth Avenue, but he always returned to the Bronx. He was a bigwig at the Cincinnati Opera House. He played Spanish barbers and mad Moroccan kings when he wasn't with us.

He was married to the diva Marilyn Kraus, and he would always bring her to our crumbling synagogue. She was a Herculean beauty, six feet tall, with the hands of a football player and a full, floating figure. When she trod up to the balcony, where all the women sat, the stairs shivered under her feet. The balcony was full of opera fans who worshiped Marilyn, called her Desdemona, and I wondered if this Desdemona was another dark lady from Belorusse.

I had the privilege of sitting with my mother and all the other women, because I was only five. Desdemona hunkered down next to us on our narrow bench, her enormous hands cradled in her lap, like a despotic queen of the balcony. She waved to the cantor, who wore a white robe and was about to wave back when he discovered the woman near his wife. The breath seemed to go out of his body. He was just like those firemen who had seen my mother for the first time. Lost in her world of letter boxes, she didn't even smile at him. The cantor was all alone; he couldn't pierce the devotion in her dark eyes. He stood among his choirboys, started to sing. But he wasn't like a postmaster dancing in slippers. He was the custodian of songs. He brought my mother out of her dream with his opening syllables. A woman swooned. I had to run and find her smelling salts . . .

He leaned against the gate with a cigarette in his mouth. A cantor wasn't allowed to smoke on the high holidays. But Rogovin could do no wrong. Desdemona wasn't with him. She must have gone back to their suite at the Concourse Plaza. My mother and I had ventured out of the synagogue with Sergeant Sam, who'd become a local hero because of his little calvaries as an air-raid warden. He was like a special policeman with a wounded face. The cantor saluted him. "Sergeant, I'd like to borrow your boy."

None of us had ever been that close to the cantor, who had little white hairs in his nose. He wore a strange perfume, smelled like a certain red flower at the Bronx Zoo.

"It's an honor," my father said. "But how can I help you? The boy is five. He doesn't have working papers. He can't spell."

"It's a sad story. My old mother has been pestering me to have a child. I had to invent one."

"You lied to her, Cantor?"

"It's scandalous. But mom's half blind, lives at a nursing home in the Bronx. Have to make mom happy before she dies."

Rogovin sobbed into his handkerchief. I'd never seen a cantor cry. His tears were the size of my mother's crystal earrings. Dad took pity on him.

"Cantor, please . . . we'll lend you the boy." He turned to my mother in bewildered fury. "Do something. We can't let the cantor choke on his tears."

I'm not sure if my mother was dreaming of Mogilev at that

moment. But she came out of her trance long enough to slap Rogovin in the face. Dad was even more perplexed. The wives of air-raid wardens weren't supposed to perform criminal acts, and assaulting cantors in a public place was worse than criminal; it was a sin against God, because God favored a cantor above all other beings. God loved a good song.

My mother slapped him again. Rogovin wasn't surprised. I saw him smile under the hand he used to cover his mouth.

My father made a fist. "I'll kill you," he said to the dark lady.

"Sergeant," the cantor said, "you shouldn't provoke Madame. She'll just go on hitting me."

"I don't understand," dad said.

"It's simple. My missus was in the balcony with Madame. They got to talking about me . . . "

"Balconies. Missus. I don't understand."

I was just as baffled. I hadn't been able to hear Desdemona whisper a word.

"Foolish," my mother said to dad. "Is no nursing home, is no blind ladies. His mother eats, drinks like a horse."

"I don't understand."

My mother seized Rogovin's thumb and placed it near her breast. "Is clear now? The cantor is lust and lecher."

Rogovin bowed to me, kissed my hand like some kind of Continental, and ran to his hotel.

My father had been so diligent in producing fur-lined vests, his boss was sending him to Florida for a week. Most wartime vacations had to be canceled, because the Army and Navy were running munitions and men on the railroads. But dad had a special pass, signed by Secretary of the Navy Frank Knox. I didn't learn about Florida until a little later—Miami Beach was a furrier's paradise, where manufacturers and their prize workers would have a yearly fling with local prostitutes and dark ladies from Havana and New Orleans. And when I grew aware of the word *prostitute*, around the age of six or seven, I understood the arguments my mother had with Sergeant Sam about his sojourns at the Flagler Hotel. She would hurl a shoe at his head, empty the perfume bottles he'd brought back from Florida, set fire to the photographs he'd hidden in some secret pocket of his valise. He'd always return terrifically tanned, looking like Clark Gable with a guilty grin.

But Gable could have been a ghost in '42. My mother didn't even watch him pack. He left in a hurry, without his air-raid warden's hat, gave me five single-dollar bills to spend in his absence, a small fortune from one of the Navy's favorite sons. I was glad to see him go. I wouldn't have to groom my mother, make her presentable to dad, hide her sorrow from him, cook his goose, load him down with whisky so he wouldn't discover her long silences.

The day he was gone her suitor arrived. I don't know what else to call him. He advertised himself as my uncle, but he didn't have our famous cheekbones and Tatar eyes. He couldn't have belonged to that tribe of Mongolian Jews who terrorized the Caucasus until they were conquered by Tamerlane the Great. Chick Eisenstadt was a big ruddy fellow who'd once worked with my mother in a Manhattan dress shop. She'd been a seamstress before she got married. The whole shop had been in love with her, according to Chick, but he was the one who linked his own history with hers long after the dress shop disappeared. He'd floundered until the war. Chick was the only one of my "relatives" who'd ever been to Sing Sing. It was convenient to have a convict in the family. He could tell you stories of the biggest outlaws. And he knew my father's timetable. He would appear whenever Sergeant Sam wasn't around.

He took us for a ride in his Cadillac. Chick wasn't supposed to have a car. Gasoline had been rationed, and there was a ban on nonessential driving. But Chick was a black marketeer who gave generals and war administrators silk stockings for their wives. He had a card that authorized him to chauffeur "essential people," like doctors and tycoons from war plants. Cops would peek into the Cadillac, glance at my mother, smile, call me "Roosevelt's little pioneer."

We crossed into Manhattan with Chick, who took me to the ocean liners that lay tilted in the harbor, like sleeping beauties with smokestacks, and I was seized with an anxiety I'd never had before. An ocean liner was larger than my imagination. It was like the imprint of a world I couldn't fathom from the Bronx. The one bridge I had was Chick.

He never bribed me, never offered expensive gifts that would have made me despise my own dad. But he took us to the only White Russian restaurant on the Grand Concourse, Bitter Eagles, where his cronies would ogle us; he'd sweat in the middle of a meal, sitting with his secret family. Sing Sing had ruined his health. He had a chronic cough, and his hands still shook from the beatings his fellow prisoners had delivered to him. Chick was thirty-five, three years older than my mother, but his hair had gone white in Sing Sing, and he looked like a war-torn cavalier.

He stared at my mother, helpless before her plate of pirogi, and said, "Faigele, what's wrong?" My mother's name was Fannie, but her admirers and friends called her Faigele, which was supposed to mean little bird in my Tatar dictionary.

"Mogilev," my mother said. One word. And Chick could intuit the entire tale.

"Your brother, the schoolteacher. His letters are no longer coming. And you're worried to death."

"The Nazis are sitting in Mogilev," I said. "Chickie, I heard it on the radio."

Chick watched my mother's grief. "Radios can lie. It's called propaganda."

"The Germans are paying the radio to tell lies?"

"I didn't say Germans. It could be the White House. And the President doesn't have to pay. Don't you get it? The President talks about a defeat that never took place. Hitler relaxes and starts to get sloppy. And we turn the tables on him."

I wouldn't argue with Chick. A black marketeer ought to know. But I didn't believe that Roosevelt would ever lie about Mogilev.

"Faigele, if there's a letter, I'll find it."

We went to the post office after lunch. The postmaster stood in his slippers, eying my mother and her black marketeer, who eyed him back.

"Mister, could one of your own men have been tampering with the mail?"

"Impossible," the postmaster said as Chick stuffed his pockets with silk stockings.

"Come on, I'll help you look for the letter. It has to be here."

They searched the back room, inspected every pouch, but there were no letters from Mogilev. "I'm sorry, Mrs. Charyn," the postmaster said. "Russian mail has been trickling in, but not a scratch from Belorusse."

Faigele took to her bed. "My two bitter eagles," she mumbled, blinking at me and Chick. It was a complete collapse. Chick's own doctor came, examined her, said he couldn't cure heartbreak and withered emotions. He recommended a rest home in the Catskills where he sent all his worst cases.

"Doc," Chick said, "she's not a case. She's a glorious woman, Faigele. She's expecting a letter from Mogilev."

"You're the wizard. You can produce silk stockings. Why not one lousy letter? But what's it all about? Did she leave a boyfriend behind?"

"A brother," Chickie said.

The doctor rolled his eyes. "Isn't it unnatural to miss a brother so much?"

Chick grabbed him by the collar, and I didn't know it then,

but it was a very brave act. This doctor was Meyer Lansky's personal physician. He'd poisoned people for the mob. He was the highest-paid internist in the Bronx.

I brought Chick and him a glass of my father's best schnapps. And then Chick explained to him the story of Faigele and Mordecai, who'd come from a family of small landowners in the Tatar town of Grodno, where Meyer Lansky was born. Mordecai was the oldest at ten, with a couple of kid sisters— Anna, five, and Faigele, two—when their mother died (their dad had run to America and made his own life). A ten-year-old boy couldn't hold on to the family fortune. He had to lease himself, become a little slave to protect his sisters. He was sold into the tzar's army at fifteen, escaped, "kidnapped" Anna and Faigele, hid out with them in the marshes, landed in Mogilev in the middle of the Russian Revolution without papers or a crust of bread. The boy was sixteen and he learned to steal. In a time of shadowlands, he became a shadow until he could reinvent himself as a schoolteacher. He had forged documents from a commissar of education who'd been killed. He had pupils in his first classes who were older than himself. He had to bribe an inspector from Minsk: it was like the tzar's government without a tzar, but the Cossacks had been told by some Soviet prince to love all the Tatar Jews. Mordecai saved his money and was able to send Anna out of Belorusse in 1923. But Faigele wouldn't go. He pleaded with her. The inspectors would catch him soon—an illiterate teacher. He couldn't breathe until his little sister was safe.

"But I am safe," she said, "here with you."

He'd start to cry, this gaunt man who was always on the verge of getting TB. She left for America in 1927. He promised to join her in six months but never did.

She became a Manhattan refugee, lived with her father and a stepmother who begrudged every bit of food she swallowed. She went to night school, worked in a dress shop, dreaming of

Mordecai. She had to get out of her father's house. Enter Sam, the furrier who never lost a day's work during the Depression.

Faigele married him, but nothing could sustain her—not children, not God, not romance—nothing except those letters that would arrive religiously from Mogilev.

The doctor licked his schnapps. "Chickie, a glorious woman, righto, but where do you fit in? You're not the husband, you're not the brother, you're not the father of this little boy."

"None of your stinking business," said Chick, already drunk. "I fill the empty spaces. I'm satisfied."

"If you want to revive her, friend, you'll just have to forge that letter . . . pretend you're with the tzar's police."

"I don't have to pretend. But how will I get Russian stamps?"

The doctor tapped my skull. "Baby, where's your mother's stash of mail?"

I steered them right to the little wooden chest my mother had brought from Belorusse; the letters were inside. Chick was mainly interested in the stamps and the quality of paper and Mordecai's penmanship, but the doctor began to read the letters in whatever Russian he still had at his command (he was born in Kiev).

"The man's a poet, Chick."

He recited from the letters, but Chick cut him off. "Keep it to yourself, doc."

"Are you insane? Poetry belongs to the world."

"But the letters belong to Faigele."

Every stamp had a different face. I saw the brown eagle of Belorusse; Tatar princes and kings; Stalin, the little father of his people, looking like a walrus. The doctor pulled a pair of scissors out of his medical bag. He wanted to cut off a few of the stamps; Chick told him to put the scissors back. He wouldn't mutilate my mother's property.

"I give up," the doctor said, while Chick and I went down to the stationery store, where I helped him pick out a blue envelope and a pad that could have passed for Russian paper. Then we walked to Bitter Eagles, found a man who was willing to trade Russian stamps in his family album for the promise of butter, eggs, and Colombian coffee.

Chick went to work practicing Mordecai's pen strokes. Time seemed to clot around him and the letter he was going to write. The doctor abandoned wife, children, mistresses, all his other patients, including Meyer Lansky, to mastermind a letter from Mogilev made in the Bronx. I brewed cups of black tea and fed them coffee cake from Bitter Eagles.

It took Chick an hour to do "Dear Faigele" in Mordecai's Russian hand and get the first paragraph going. They had to tiptoe around the war because Chick wouldn't load the letter with lurid details. "I am only starving a little bit," he wrote in schoolteacher Russian and signed Mordecai's name. He addressed the envelope, I glued on the stamps, and we all fell asleep in the living room on different chairs.

A knocking sound came right through my dreams. I got up, stumbled to the door. The postmaster stood in his slippers with a letter in his hand. He was very excited. "Gentlemen, it arrived, right out of the blue." Chick offered him some of our fabulous coffee cake, speckled with dark chocolate. "Delicious," he said. No one thanked him for the letter, which had come in a crumpled white envelope, all the stamps missing. The postmaster left. Chick tore up *our* letter and we went in to wake up my mother and give her the other letter from Mogilev.

She danced out of bed like a mermaid with a nightgown on (I'd never seen a mermaid, so I had to imagine one). She savored the letter, but she wouldn't read it until she prepared our tea. The doctor was startled by her metamorphosis. Faigele's coloring had come back. She disappeared into the bedroom and closed the door.

"The angels would be envious of such a creature," the

doctor said.

We waited like orphans until my mother came out. She wouldn't share Mordecai's language with us. "Is still schoolteacher," she said, summarizing the plot. "But without school. Was bombed."

The doctor returned to his practice. Chickie had to go out of town. My father got back from Miami with his movie-star tan, but Faigele was the one who had all the flush. He put on his air-raid helmet and patrolled the streets. I imagined him in the blackout, looking for renegade cubes of light. Poor Sergeant Sam, who could never really capture the dark lady, or her radiance.

Bambi

It was after she heard from Mordecai that my mother began to notice me again. "Baby, you look so thin." She woke from her bout of amnesia and remembered that she hadn't shopped in a month. Baby had done all the marketing. I had to pay the butcher out of my mother's purse, use my fingers as an abacus, teach myself to bargain like a tycoon. I still couldn't spell or master long and short division. The war was turning me into an ignoramus, and the dark lady took my education into her own hands. If the Bronx couldn't supply a kindergarten, she would create one.

We taught each other how to spell. She'd been the princess of her class at night school, dreamt of becoming a scientist, like Madame Curie. She still had the dog-eared copy of *Bambi* her class had given her as a wedding present. We sought refuge in the book. That forest of talking animals and pesty little birds took us out of the Bronx, and bit by bit Faigele began to recall the prickly landscape of English she'd lost after night school.

We had to sight each word, sound it on our tongues, before it would give up any secret. Words would float along a line like ships caught in a white sea, and you had to lend yourself to them like a sea captain, or you'd never learn to read. We spent a week traveling across the first page, and we had our own compass (a dictionary I'd found in a garbage barrel), but the compass was a tricky one, almost as hard to read as *Bambi* itself until we grasped some of its signs. And then it steered us into the book, and we both began to cry, because it was a powerful elixir to read about a baby deer and his mom who could have been Faigele and me.

When Bambi's mom was killed by hunters who were known as "He," both of us had to stop reading for a month. We couldn't go on with the story, even with our compass. My father caught us moping. "Crazyheads," he called us. "Only crazyheads would believe what's written in a book."

Dad wasn't a reader. He couldn't understand how anyone could mourn people on a page. But Bambi and her mom were dearer to us than our own blood and bones. And when our mourning period was over, we went back to the book, digging cautiously at the words, since we were beginners and could only deal with a bit of heartbreak at a time. We went through the motions of keeping house for Sergeant Sam, but we belonged to Bambi. And it's cruel to say, but I didn't see any resemblance between my dad and Bambi's, the old Prince of the forest who was aloof to everyone, yet adored Bambi at a distance. With his helmet and his armband and his military bearing, Sam could have been one of the hunters who crushed the forest animals or trained them as pets. In my own mind, he was a man with a gun.

Mom and I were delirious when Bambi beat the heck out of a young buck and started going steady with Faline. Faigele would laugh and search my crown for bumps.

"Where are the antlers of Jerome?"

But I couldn't grow horns. I was a little boy who had to crawl with Faigele through his first book. Bambi exhausted us; we were irritable at the end. We didn't have the stamina to start another book, and our souls were still deep inside the forest. I'd watch Faigele light a cigarette and scan the book, let it fly to whatever page it wanted, and chant to herself. "Bambi braced with his hind legs and hurled himself at Ronni [one of the bucks who was interested in Faline]."

"Mama," I said, "what is *braced?*"

"Metal . . . to help your mouth."

"But a deer couldn't go to the dentist, mama."

"Then is a mystery."

"Couldn't we ask Chick?"

My "uncle" had stopped calling on us. He knew that dad was back in harness as an air-raid warden. And Chick had never liked to sneak around in the bushes. If he couldn't come in his Cadillac, he wouldn't come at all. It was frustrating as hell to have a part-time uncle who was kind to you a couple of weeks a year: Chickie, who was like the old Prince of the forest, nice and proud, but with ration books instead of antlers.

Mom wouldn't have given in and gone to Chick, but she was curious about the word *braced*. She started fixing herself in the mirror, with every little tube that could color your face, and we went downstairs and walked to Bitter Eagles. It was an hour after the big White Russian lunch. Bitter Eagles had emptied out. A hurricane could have gripped the restaurant. There weren't any pirogi or pickled cabbage inside the steam table. The black chocolate coffee cake was gone. A hundred empty tea glasses sat in their silver holders near gutted pots of strawberry jam. Behind the silver holders, at a separate table, was Chick, staring at some void until my mother came in. It wasn't the same Chick who could write a letter from Mogilev. He had stubble on his chin. His white hair wasn't combed. It might not have been noticeable in another man. But Chick had his suits made at Feuerman & Marx (the most aristocratic uptown tailor), and he looked like a vagabond if even one of his shoes wasn't shined.

He danced out from behind the table in a Feuerman suit that had buttons with orange veins. The handkerchief in his coat was also orange. His cufflinks had painted orange borders. "Faigele, is your sergeant somewhere at sea?"

"Is not about a sailor," she said, putting *Bambi* on the table. Chick shouted at the waiter until glasses of bloodred tea appeared with the last Russian coffee cake in the Bronx. Then he sat down again, turned to the book with its broken spine and faded image of Bambi on the cover with antlers like a crown of bony knives and forks.

"Helluva book. Read it to my daughters."

What daughters? Chick had never discussed any daughters in front of me. I took it like a slap. He must have had a wife when he first met Faigele, a wife and a daughter or two, and that's why mom had never married him.

She showed him *our* sentence from the book.

"Braced," he muttered. Chick had gone to law school and dropped out after a year. His biggest diploma, he liked to say, had come from Sing Sing.

"Chickie, doesn't the President have a leg brace?"

"Roosevelt has nothing to do with this . . . Bambi can brace himself, tighten the screws in his legs. But the difference between Roosevelt and a deer is night and day."

"Braces are braces," I said, and at least I got him to laugh. Chick was our local Robin Hood who gouged the rich and gave to the poor. He didn't exactly give. He charged the poor cut-rate prices, sold them tubs of butter at cost. But he'd interfered with another Robin Hood, Darcy Staples, a dentist who was attached to Ed Flynn, boss of the Bronx. Darcy was Flynn's lieutenant, an under-chief who ruled the Grand Concourse like his own kingdom, an Irish Protestant in a sea of Jews. He kept an office at the Darcy Arms, a mecca he'd built in his own name. The mecca had already collapsed once. It was made of steel wool and rusty wires and a kind of cheesecake cement. Rats ate the steel wool in the walls and bled out their entrails in Darcy's cellar. He was in the business of ration stamps and wartime contraband, like Chick. They were often partners. But Darcy had decided to punish Chick. Was it greed or jealousy or plain spite? A boy of five couldn't have read such rivalries. Darcy was holding an important shipment of ration books and squeezing Chick to death. He claimed the government was watching his office, and he couldn't move the stamps. Chickie would have to collect them himself.

"He'll murder me, Faigele. He's that kind of man."

"But he wouldn't dare to murder me."

"Why not?"

"He's my dentist."

Darcy was everybody's dentist. Patients would come from Westchester and Long Island to sit in Darcy's chair. That was his advantage. All his deals were made with the smell of ether and chloroform hanging over you. He could dope his enemies and get rid of them, or fill a friend with laughing gas. Darcy's office was the real hub of the Bronx. Boss Flynn would appear with his retinue. He was FDR's point man on the East Coast. He left Darcy to deal with mundane matters. Darcy's gang would break a couple of heads when they had to. Most of the men on his payroll were cops who did a little moonlighting for their dentist. He was my dentist too. And he'd give me special candy that didn't rot your teeth. He was a handsome man with silver hair. I didn't love Darcy the way I loved Chick, but I never had as much fun as the time I spent in Darcy's chair. Darcy caressed my mouth with a long metal toothpick, and its curled head would make a gentle noise against my teeth. He wouldn't fob me off on any of his assistants. I was little Charyn, who had the dark lady as his private kindergarten teacher.

We went to Darcy without an appointment, because otherwise we'd have had to wait for weeks. "Faigele," Chick had told us. "I'd like to blow up Darcy's cheesebox one of these days . . . don't spar with him. Be direct. Ask him for Chickie's merchandise." But it wasn't that simple. Darcy's cheesebox sat near the Bronx County Building. And there was a constant flow of traffic between the county court and Darcy's office. Every single judge who wanted to insure his future had to consult with the dentist. And so we sat with judges and police captains in Darcy's outer room, while his own lieutenants picked their teeth. We were eleventh or twelfth in line, but when Darcy

popped his head out of his private office, he ignored the judges and motioned to us. I ran right in and jumped on the chair,
which was older than Darcy and Boss Flynn and had to be
lowered and raised with a little wheel.

"Ah, Mrs. C, it's a pleasure. Does the little one have a toothache? . . . Baby, open your mouth."

"Is a different toothache," my mother said.

"Then sit down with Baby, and I'll administer to both of
you."

"Doctor, is Chick who has the ache."

The dentist lost a bit of his gaiety. "He's a genius, then.
Hires you as his camel."

"Yes," my mother said. "I am the camel."

It was a Bronx term, used by black marketeers. A camel carried contraband in one or two of his humps.

"I envy Chick. But it's a pleasure doing business with a camel
like you."

"Is treasury agents in other office?"

"Wouldn't pollute my own practice, would I now? What
would my patients think?"

"Tell me Chick's sin."

"He's working his own charities in my yard. Undercutting
my prices. Selling wares only to unfortunate people who nurse
their misfortune at my expense. They can go into business for
themselves, considering what Chickie charges. I'm the warden
here, I'm the bishop. I set the ceiling and I set the floor on
each article, not Chick. And you had better instruct him, dear
Faigele."

"I will instruct," mom said, like a shrewd kindergarten teacher.

And Darcy gave her a shoebox filled with ration books that
she didn't have to hide in any hump. This shoebox was the
dentist's particular mark. There were hardly any briefcases in
the Bronx. Leather couldn't be found in 1942. It was on the
list of rationed goods. And lawyers at the courthouse began

to copy from that prince of the Grand Concourse. They carried their files in a shoebox secured with a rubber band. Rubber was also rationed, and the lawyers' rubber bands were as precious as milk and meat and gold.

We returned to Bitter Eagles with the shoebox. Chick went out of his mind. He danced on the tables and drank vodka in the afternoon. His white hair shone in the dark corners under the ceiling. "Ah, my little ones," he said from his perch, kissing the shoebox like a crazyman. "We'll rejoice together, or my name isn't Chick."

"What rejoice? I have to wash potatoes, prepare Sam's stew."

"Faigele, I insist."

"Insist," mom said, "but you don't have husband who eats like a horse."

"Darling, I'll ask the chef to fix him a meal."

"Don't darling so much."

"Ah, it was a slip of the tongue," Chick said, coming down off the tables and leading us to the door. He let me hold the shoebox while he wobbled in the street. Mom could never be ashamed of Chickie. She took him by the arm, steadied Chick, and we sailed across the Grand Concourse with the wind on our backs and stopped at a certain marquee.

We weren't dumb, Faigele and I. You could get an awful lot from the radio. *Bambi* had been turned into a picture, but how could we know it was Hollywood's biggest hit? When we caught that name on the marquee, we didn't even smile. It was as if the territory of our book had been invaded, had been pulled from our hands. We went inside with Chick.

And when we saw Bambi on the screen, both of us were alarmed, because we knew his mom's fate. The forest was thick and dark, a hiding place for hunters and their dogs. Bambi's mom disappeared from the picture, but we couldn't cry. We'd been mourning her from the first image.

Chick seemed to grasp our long silence. "Gorgeous," he

said, "but it could never hold a candle to the book." And we walked home without him. The picture must have marked us, because it felt like we were up on the screen, waiting for the hunters to arrive. And they did. They attacked Chick, took his bundle of ration books, robbed him right outside Bitter Eagles, beat him up, four men wearing handkerchief masks tucked under their eyes. No one would talk about them, but they couldn't have fallen from the sky. Their swagger was perilously close to the policemen who moon-lighted for the dentist. Darcy had taken Chick out of the black-marketing business. But he was still our prince, and he paid for Chickie's room at Cedars of Lebanon. That's how one Robin Hood behaved with another.

Faigele and I had to sneak into the hospital when Chickie's wife and daughters weren't around. Mom didn't like to play the hidden bombshell, but she was fond of Chick. And she wouldn't desert him when he was riding on some hospital bed, in a somber sea, with black marks under his eyes. His white hair had begun to yellow. He had bandages on his nose and mouth. Mom had cooked a coffee cake in her oven, with almonds and the dark chocolate that Chickie loved. He stuffed a morsel under his bandage. "Piquant," he said.

It was hard for Chickie to talk, but I had to ask him something. "What's *piquant?*"

"Tart and tasty," he said.

And we had to leave before his wife arrived. I was learning more and more about her. She was a holy terror named Marsha who'd gone to Hunter College and become an English teacher at William Howard Taft, the high school that belonged to the Grand Concourse. The whole school was afraid of her. Marsha had a big mouth. She could sing reprimands while she recited some great poet out of the past. I envied Marsha, mistress of the English language, and worried about meeting her. What would she do to mom and me with a tongue that was so powerful and piquant?

But we met a different monster outside Chickie's room. Darcy Staples, wearing a silk scarf and a coat with a fur collar, and carrying a bunch of cornflowers shaped like the devil's ears. He'd come with his usual band, a judge and three cops.

"Morning, Faigele . . . ah, you've already seen Chick. A terrible accident. Four lubbards taking advantage of a businessman. Out-of-town boys, they were. They'll be punished. I've spread the word."

Mom took out her handkerchief, folded it like a mask, and put it on in front of the dentist.

"Darcy, am I out-of-town boy?" she said, and steered me to the door. But we couldn't escape Bambi's forest. The hunters' hounds must have tracked us home. Sergeant Sam was lying in bed with a woeful look and a very fat bandage that covered his hand like a boxing glove; the bandage was tinged with blood. In a rush to meet some admiral's demand for fur-lined vests, dad had nearly cut off his thumb. He'd have to be replaced as foreman at his own shop while the thumb healed. The War Department couldn't wait for Sergeant Sam. Meanwhile he could collect workman's compensation, but it was a pittance compared to all the extras he usually got. Something else ate at Sam. He'd let down all the admirals with a stupid accident. He'd been sculpting fur collars much too fast, had sabotaged his own hand with a wickedly sharp knife.

He got out of bed after a week to put on his warden's hat. Dad made his rounds with that bloody boxing glove, which he had to wear in a sling while he clutched an enormous flashlight in his one free hand. He must have had a romantic air in the dark winter light, because people began to call him the Count of Monte Cristo. But dad wasn't feeling romantic. Phantoms had begun to invade his head. They told him he'd be fired, that he'd never be foreman again. Not even the Christmas bonus his boss had sent him could soothe Sergeant

Sam. It was only a kiss-off, he said, a sign that they were getting rid of him. "Baby, I'm dying. Hold my hand."

I held his hand. "Dad, dad, it isn't true."

But he slipped into a morbidity that paralyzed him. I had to comb his hair, help him put on his metal hat, or he wouldn't have made his rounds as an air-raid warden. Where was Faigele? He'd fallen outside her affections. The dark lady couldn't seem to lend him the least bit of her heart. I accompanied Sam to his headquarters, a storefront on Sheridan Avenue that every-body called the Church. There was nothing churchlike about it. It had a long, dirty window shade that blocked out all the light. I felt like I was descending into the mouth of a cave. There were calendars of naked women on the wall, but I couldn't really catch much more than a general blondness and one or two brown nipples. The Church had a sofa without any cushions, a lamp that barely lit up its own outline, a couple of chairs, a gunmetal gray filing cabinet and desk. A woman tended the desk. She must have been some kind of dispatcher. She had short hair and chubby fingers and she smoked cigars like a man. Her name was Miriam, and she was very fat. She kept a map of our district over her desk; all the streets looked like little dark canals.

"Charyn," she said, with the glowing ashes of her cigar like a raw red wound in the cave's particular midnight. "I can fill in with another soldier. You don't have to trouble your bad hand."

"Baby will walk with me," dad said.

Two other wardens came into the Church, carrying big sacks on their shoulders. They saluted Sergeant Sam and emptied their sacks on the desk. I couldn't make out all the objects, but I could swear I saw a radio and some toasters. These men were camels with metal hats. They were taking advantage of the blackout to move merchandise around. And I wondered if they were also burglars. They could have climbed through a ground-floor window in the dark, pillaged a couple of living rooms on their rounds.

"A poor crop," the first one said to Miriam.

"Jackie, you shouldn't advertise yourself in front of the boy."

"Baby's all right," the second one said.

I went outside with Sam, propped the flashlight against my hip and pointed it at the roofs, while dad looked straight ahead. The Count of Monte Cristo.

He was just as melancholy in the morning. He wouldn't move. There was a long river of sadness that seemed to run right through his side of the family. A grandfather who ate the bitter ground at some backwoods asylum. Cousins who died of convulsions. I couldn't coax Sam out of bed. I had to go to Cedars of Lebanon with the dark lady.

Chick was in a panic. "The dentist cleaned out all my goods. I don't have a single tub of butter left . . . or a lousy silk stocking."

"So you'll be naked. But how did dentist know where to look?"

"Faigele," Chick said behind his mask of bandages. "The whole inventory was at Bitter Eagles. In a back room."

"Is black market? I will never eat again."

But we went to Darcy's cheesebox. The dentist took us right away. He didn't even ask me to sit in his chair.

"Shall we do some business, dear Faigele?"

"Is monkey business, Darcy dear. I would like you not to be such a dybbuk. Give back what belongs to the man in the hospital bed."

"I'll hound him into the grave . . . until you come and work for me."

"You need a dental assistant to dance without clothes?"

"I'm not that fond of cabaret," Darcy said. "I run a card game. It's strictly legal. I have judges, barbers, and the borough president at my Monday-afternoon games."

"And should I serve sandwiches?"

"I want you to deal the cards for me."

"I'm not a gambler."

"That's the whole point," Darcy said. "The men will trust you. A beautiful woman with a five-year-old tot."

"Is soon six."

"That's colossal. Bring Baby along. I don't want professionals. I want a woman who can look those men right in the eye, even if she deals them a pair of deuces all night."

"Is an afternoon game."

"I was only taking liberties with the language, dear Faigele, not with you. Your husband's sick. I can't cure him, but I can offer you a hundred dollars for each afternoon, and I will personally cart Chick's stuff back to that stinking restaurant of his."

"Is White Russian, best food in the world."

"Wouldn't demean the menu, would I? But will you work for me?"

"And you will make the whole Bronx not to bother Chick?"

"On my life."

"Then I will deal cards for you . . . but what is a pair of deuces?"

Darcy laughed. "Lord, I am in love with this woman." He dismissed his other patients, herded them out of the office, and we spent the afternoon playing poker in Darcy's private salon.

I wasn't with the dark lady at all her poker lessons. I had to take care of dad. She cooked for him, changed his bandages, fell asleep with him in the same bed, but her spirit seemed worlds away from Sergeant Sam. Mom had fattened her vocabulary at my expense. Darcy was teaching her all the language of a croupier. She could count and distribute chips, fling cards across a velvet tablecloth, and snap out a little song with every card she delivered. "Possible straight flush . . . pair of aces . . . full house."

Mom brought me along to the first poker game. She was wearing a blue dress. The gamblers couldn't keep their eyes off Faigele. "Jesus," said Fred R. Lions, our borough president. "Darcy, you broke my heart. You can't bring your own weapon to the game. It isn't fair. I'll never see my way to a royal flush with her around."

"Should I change the dealer, Mr. Lions?"

"I'll rip out your lungs. She'll deal for us until eternity."

"She's not a circus animal, Mr. Lions. She's Faigele, and you'll please address her as such."

"Faigele, Faigele," mumbled the president of the Bronx. "She's Joan Crawford, or else I'm a blind man."

"Crawford, Joan Crawford," the other gamblers said.

"She's Faigele. I wouldn't have Joan Crawford in this house. And the child is little Charyn, known as Baby to his friends."

But Fred R. Lions wasn't so wrong. Mom could have passed for Joan Crawford's younger twin. Both of them were dark ladies. One was born Lucille Le Sueur in San Antonio, Texas. The other was born Fannie Paley in Belorusse. One was the pony in a chorus line and a card dealer in Detroit before she grew into the dark lady of MGM. The other was an orphan who was practicing her English at the most aristocratic card game in the Bronx.

Darcy liked to say I was his sheriff who rode shotgun for Faigele. But mom didn't need a sheriff. I sat on a tall stool with its very own ladder that allowed me to climb up and down at will. I ate a lot of potato chips. I answered the telephone for Darcy. I opened each fresh deck of cards, tearing off the cellophane with my teeth, while mom smoked cigarette after cigarette, and held that game together with the force of her own dark eyes. She'd slap a hand when she had to.

"Don't peek at neighbors' cards, Judge John."

No one contested her, no one griped. The game was Faigele's. And soon people were fighting for a seat around the

poker table. The gamblers always tipped her, always left my
mother some largesse. I was elected to carry twists of five- and
ten-dollar bills inside my shirt pocket. We were almost growing
rich in that second winter of the war. Sergeant Sam could sit
home with his damaged thumb. We didn't have to depend on
workman's compensation.

My mother had become partners with Chick. He had no
one else to move his merchandise. She would go from the card
game to Bitter Eagles in the borough president's black limousine, and she'd have to tell all of Chickie's camels (housewives
and retired furriers) what to deliver and where. The chef fixed
a late-afternoon box lunch, which she brought to Cedars of
Lebanon, with Baby at her side. I smuggled splits of champagne into the hospital in one of Darcy's shoeboxes.

He was almost healed, Faigele's black marketeer. The bandages had come off his nose and mouth. The bruises under his
eyes were now a pale green. He had only one soft scar on his
lip. We closed the door of Chickie's room and climbed onto
the bed with him. I poured champagne. We had caviar that
looked like the crimson seeds of a Chinese apple. Mom toast-
ed blinis on the radiator. We had Russian coffee cake with the
hospital's tepid tea. Faigele was tipsy, not from champagne, but
from all the nervous energy, after having to control a roomful
of gamblers. Her eyes began to flutter. She hugged Chick and
me. She would have danced with us on the bed, done some
crazy Bronx cancan, but the door opened, and a woman came
in, near my mother's age, with a long nose and the unremarkable features of an old maid. She was clutching her own lunch
basket and two girls with long noses and unremarkable eyes. I
didn't need much imagination to guess who they were. Marsha
Eisenstadt, the holy terror of William Howard Taft, with her
daughters, Cordelia and Annabel Lee.

Chick was terrified, but I watched him gather his wits like
any good businessman. "Marsha," he said, "come and meet my

associate, Mrs. Paley Charyn."

"The Park Avenue Paleys?" Marsha asked.

"No. Sheridan Avenue and Belorusse."

"Ah, that Paley Charyn, the card dealer, with her own illiterate boy."

"It's wartime," my mother said, pulling all her grammar
together. "The kindergartens are closed. Please don't insult my
son."

Marsha looked at my mother and realized that she wasn't
another Bronx bombshell her husband had picked up on one
of his black-marketing trails. The dark lady had destabilized her.
Marsha's engine had broken down. Faigele was outside the
harm of her vocabulary.

She said, "Bastards and bums," which didn't sound much like
an educated lady. And she left with her daughters, who hadn't
even kissed their dad.

"Faigele," Chick said, "I swear, it's only a marriage of con-
venience."

Mom began to collect the debris of our meal. She dropped
the empty splits into the shoebox, put the remains of the caviar
inside Chick's night table. "And what other kind of marriages
are there?"

"Marrying you," Chick said.

"And we would have lived in the forest with Bambi and all
the black marketeers."

We walked out with the shoebox and never saw Chickie at
the hospital again.

Ringworm

It was considered the Bronx disease. I'm not sure why. But every time you noticed a boy wearing a big hat in the thick of summer or spring, you could always tell what the hat meant. Ringworm. Blisters that would erupt on your scalp like the circular mouths of a volcano. But this volcano had nothing but skin inside and a crust that was shaped like Saturn's rings. And the rings themselves resembled horrible, lifeless pink worms. Polio might cripple you, but ringworm marked you as an outcast. You couldn't walk into school with such a big hat hiding a shaved head. You had to remain on furlough until the blisters healed.

I pitied the boys with ringworm, and kept away from them. I was storing up my future, waiting for September and the beginning of the school year, when I could waltz right into the first grade. Mom still loved books, but she couldn't keep up with our kindergarten classes while she was dealing cards and supervising Chick's camels. The load of my education fell upon dad, who couldn't really read or write. And I taught dad how to read while he was teaching me. That was the planet of the Paley Charyns, which always moved in reverse from every other planet.

Dad would bathe his thumb in a solution of Epsom salts, and he didn't have to wear that boxing glove, but he seemed terrified to return to his shop. What ghosts could there have been waiting downtown at the fur market? Mom offered to take him there, but dad declined. "Go to your camels," he said. "Baby will bring me."

And that's how I had my first subway ride. A few days before I was six. Dad and I were both dressed in brown. We looked like a couple of soldiers. I loved being under the ground. The lights in the subway car would start to blink, and I made a wish: I wanted to move into the tunnels, live there, among the rats, without mother or father, or a room of my own, neither a Paley nor a Charyn, just a rat boy with no connections. But it didn't happen.

We got out of the subway at Pennsylvania Station, and I couldn't get used to the raw daylight. It ripped at my eyes. I walked like a blind man. But I couldn't desert my dad. We crossed a big street and rode up an elevator, stepped out in front of a metal door with a sign in the middle. I could gobble each let-ter— R-O-Y-A-L F-U-R C-O-R-P-O-R-A-T-I-O-N— because I already knew the name of dad's shop. I jumped into the air, hit the buzzer, and went through the door with dad. My whole head began to ring. I'd never seen such a racket coming out of one place. The factory floor rocked under my feet. Men and women were sitting around an enormous table, shouting, cursing, sneezing, mimicking each other, while they tore at bolts of cloth with knives and shears, and flung these mutilated articles at other men and women, who caught them in midair and thrust them under the driving needles of sev-eral sewing machines. But the fury stopped the moment all these men and women saw Sam. They abandoned their tools and got up from the table to shake my father's hand and stare at me.

"The little man of the house," dad said. "Baby. I have to watch him since they closed the kindergartens."

"Who closed the kindergartens?"

"The bosses of the Bronx," dad said. "They're saving money, putting it into their own pockets."

"But we can teach him a trade. The union will have to let in a boy who lost his kindergarten."

A big fat lady sat me in her lap, and I lived between her heart and her sewing machine. I couldn't operate the treadle. My legs were too small. But I could clutch a piece of cloth in my fists, guide it under the fangs of the machine, and watch it grow into half a vest. I never saw one finished article at dad's factory, or the skin of a single silver fox. Fur must have been as hard to find as shoe leather. But how could the factory make fur-lined vests? I asked the fat lady.

"It's a military secret," she said.

The boss had gone to Washington to meet with Navy big-wigs at the War Department, but dad didn't need instructions from him. He put on a blue apron and profited from his visit to the factory. Winking at the women, encouraging the men, he danced around the table and ruled each sewing machine at the Royal fur shop. Without his melancholia, dad was Clark Gable again.

And I stayed home while dad went to work. I inherited his morbidity. Mom had her new vocation, dad had his shop and his duties as a warden, and I had nothing but a dog-eared book. I couldn't feed forever on deer in the forest. I had to make my own life, but I didn't even have a school to go to.

I began to pester mom. I caught her in the middle of pre-paring her eyes and mouth for the poker game.

"Mom, don't you have to register me for the first grade?"

"I registered you for kindergarten, and look what happened."

"But how will I get to school?"

"I'll bring you in July and ask to see the principal."

"Faigele, the schools are closed in July."

"Then we'll find another solution," mom said, and we ran down to the dentist to meet our fate with a deck of cards. The dark lady had become much more than a dealer. She would accompany Fred. R. Lions to the Concourse Plaza after the game. Sometimes Darcy was there, sometimes he wasn't. But the Concourse Plaza was where Mr. Lions held court. He didn't have Darcy's silver look. He was a sloppy little guy with a homburg and a rumpled black suit. He kept mothballs in his pockets. He wasn't a black marketeer like the dentist, and he couldn't have gotten elected without Boss Flynn, but he was the Bronx's very own bagman. He collected whatever money was owed to the borough chiefs, calling on Darcy's muscle when he had to, and dispensing small favors from his crimson chair, like some kind of cut-rate pope. And the dark lady lent a touch of glamour to Mr. Lions.

Darcy had hired mom to sit with our borough president and keep him sober. Mom had to memorize his accounts, because a bagman couldn't afford to practice his penmanship and leave a paper trail. She softened his truculence, prevented him from doing damage to Darcy's machine.

America had two wartime capitals: the Bronx and Washington, DC. FDR ruled the country from his wheelchair at the White House, but it was Boss Flynn who kept him there, who brought out the voters, and held the other bosses in line. "Manhattan?" Lions loved to growl, like Boss Flynn's private little parrot. "Ain't that where the Republicans live?"

Manhattan had a Republican mayor, LaGuardia, but Flynn had banished him from the Bronx. He boycotted City Hall, treated the Bronx like his own enclave. He didn't require any largesse from Fiorello LaGuardia. He had FDR on his side, and he had his own army. Policemen, firemen, and garbagemen in the Bronx were loyal to Flynn. How many people would dare oppose a man who had his own bed at the White House, who played poker with FDR? Even LaGuardia listened to Flynn, and stayed out of the Bronx . . . leaving it to Mr. Lions.

He was a bachelor with his own suite at the Concourse Plaza. His neighbors were the New York Yankees, who lived at the hotel during the baseball season (Yankee Stadium was right down the hill).

Photo

Gallery

Mordecai, 1937.

Faigele (left) and three companions,
Belorusse, circa 1926.

Faigele between two friends, Coney Island, circa 1929.

The Paley sisters, Anna (left) and Faigele (right), 1930.

Harvey and Faigele, 1935.

Harvey in his Sea Scout uniform, 1944.

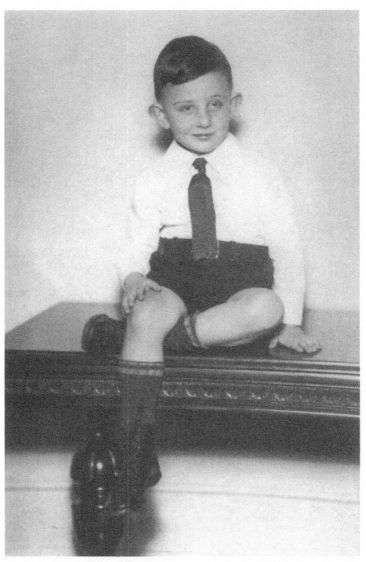
Baby, just before this story begins.

Sam and Faigele, 1933.

Everybody searched for Joe DiMaggio, but Joe had gone off to the war, and we had to be satisfied with Charlie "King Kong" Keller, the only slugger the Yanks had left. Keller had become the main attraction at the Concourse Plaza. Guests would hover close to him, shout "King Kong," and beg for his autograph. And that's the real reason Darcy had to hire mom—not to baby-sit for a borough president, but to counter "King Kong."

The dark lady began to attend more and more functions in the Bronx with Darcy and Mr. Lions. She couldn't take me along to a banquet or a midnight supper honoring Boss Flynn. Dad would often have dinner at the fur market, and like a forest animal, I learned how to fend for myself. I had to stand on a kitchen ladder if I wanted to cook some chocolate pudding. And because I'd been so busy with mom, and had to suffer without a kindergarten, I didn't make any friends. I felt like a frozen child who could only come to life once school began. I bought myself a pencil case, a fat box of crayons, a jar of white paste. I watched the calendar like a hawk. I couldn't afford to let time jump backward and play a trick on me.

But there were more than calendar tricks. One night, when dad wasn't working overtime, and the dark lady wasn't at some bazaar with Mr. Lions, and we were all at the dinner table, dad drank too much whisky and picked a fight with mom. It could have been about Mr. Lions and Darcy and mom's camels, or dad's girlfriends in Miami and at his shop.

"That dentist," dad said, "and his band of thieves." Dad was a member of the Liberal Party, which broke with the Democrats to help elect LaGuardia.

"Fiorello can't show his face in the Bronx."

"Why should he?" dad said. "You have nothing to see but black marketeers."

In their fury they began to hurl dishes at each other. But their fight wasn't about Fiorello, the Little Flower. Mom and dad had traveled outside each other's orbit, and they couldn't find their way back.

It was dad who tossed the last dish. He must have sensed the futility, because he smiled like Clark Gable, looked at the fallout in my hair, blue and white shrapnel from the broken dishes, and offered to take us to the movies. We left the shrapnel on our shoulders and traveled around the corner to watch a war movie, *The Immortal Sergeant*, at the Luxor. It was about British commandos in desert country. I remember the grease on their faces, the netting that covered their helmets, and fortunes of sand.

And I remember our own immortal sergeant grabbing my arm after the movies and asking, "Baby, who do you love more, mom or me?"

We were like bitter commandos standing in the street, without a desert to hide in. I'd been around Darcy and Mr. Lions long enough. I knew about politics. All I had to say was, *Dad, I love you both*. But I couldn't. I was frightened of losing the dark lady.

Dad asked me again. "Who do you love more?"

"Mom," I said. "Faigele."

I dreamt of the desert, without commandos or camels, just hills that looked like the Bronx. And I was one lone boy in a warden's hat, condemned to climbing those hills, with crayons in my pocket and a little pot of glue that leaked out of my pants, like the sticky elements of my own future.

Dad never talked about that conversation outside the Luxor, but I knew he'd bear a grudge against me for life. I'd landed on the far side of his affections, become a stranger in his house. The son of an air-raid warden, I stopped accompanying dad on his rounds, couldn't even carry his flashlight, search the roofs for saboteurs, like Nazi dwarfs who dropped from the sky after sailing across the Atlantic in tiny balloons.

I held close to *Bambi's* printed lines, lived in the white spaces between every word, sweated like a tailor to build my own vocabulary. I had to be prepared for the first grade. I still sat on a stool while the dark lady dealt aces and kings, I still followed her to the Concourse Plaza, but I kept imagining what it would be like to sit in a classroom with children my own age, who wouldn't keep blabbering about royal flushes and black-market butter.

I got through June and July, and then, around the second week of August, my scalp started to itch. Mom caught me scratching, said I had the hives. "It's a weakness the Paleys have. When we're nervous about something, we break out in a rash."

"I'm not nervous, mom."

"Yes you are. You're frightened of the first grade."

The itching got worse. I tore at my own head. Soon my scalp was bleeding. Mom would slap my hands. "Baby, don't you dare." But it didn't matter what I did. My hair started to fall out. Six years old, and I already had a bald spot. Mom dragged me to the doctor. It was the same jovial man who had helped Chick write that letter from Mogilev. Meyer Lansky's personal physician. His name was Katz. He looked at my scalp with a fluorescent lamp that he carried like a torch. I cried when he put on a pair of white gloves and shaved my head. I could see my own round, red sores in the mirror. It was the Bronx plague.

"Ringworm doesn't run in the family," mom said. "The boy is clean. I scrub him with my hands twice a week."

"Faigele, it's a fungus. Could happen to any kid."

"In orphanages, yes. And playgrounds. In summer camps. But the boy doesn't know how to play. He's a bookworm."

"Mom, I'm the only bookworm who can't read."

The doctor bathed my scalp in a black lotion that stank of tar. Then he wrapped my head in gauze and lent me a baseball cap to wear. But the cap couldn't hide my baldness, nothing could.

The news spread like a crazy fire. Our neighbors tried to be nice, but they wouldn't let their own children near me. Other kids hurled water bombs from windows and roofs, shouting "Ringworm, Ringworm." The bombs were made of cardboard, and when they exploded, the noise nearly broke your eardrums. But my biggest trouble came from the Bronx Seabees, a gang of eight- and nine-year-olds who worshiped the Navy and wanted to build battleships and pontoon harbors and bridges. Meanwhile they took it upon themselves to build a harbor out of my hide. They would steal my hats, oblige me to run through a gauntlet of broomsticks and Seabee "bats," which consisted of rolled-up newspaper, tightened with bands of wire. They would whack my shoulders, legs, and bottom, while I covered my baldness and endured the wire's bite.

Their leaders were the Rathcart twins, Newton and Val, redheads with a mean streak and a fabulous IQ. They lived at the Albatross, a housing development for rich people. The Albatross had a central garden and a gate with gold spears. Newton and Val's mom was a world-famous artist, Rosemund Rathcart, who had her own comic strip in the *Daily Mirror*. It was called "Rat Man," and it was about a dishonorably discharged marine, Private Launcelot Perry, who's down and out in Shark Bay, a town that had all the earmarks of the Bronx—a boulevard like the Grand Concourse, a borough hall, a ballpark, a botanical garden. Launcelot Perry sold hot dogs at the ballpark, and lived among the rats, behind a garbage barrel. His fiancée was a nurse, Emma Martins, who tried to redeem the rat man, bring him back to civilization. Launcelot Perry didn't want to get civilized. But that didn't make him any less of a patriot. After the war started, Launcelot began to collect Germans and Japs who were coming in off the bay and skulking around in the tunnels under the ballpark. The Army and the Navy kept offering him a big reward, but the rat man wouldn't grab their money, or go back into the Marines as a lance corporal. He was happy selling hot dogs.

I couldn't read most of the balloons that went with the comic strip, but I saw enough to realize that no one would ever move me as much as the rat man, Launcelot Perry. I was hooked on him for life. He was outside the trap of politics and wealth. The rat man had no aspirations. He wouldn't have been chasing spies if there had been no war.

The rat man's mama, Rosemund, had agreed to conduct art classes at Adath Israel, that temple on the Grand Concourse. She was helping out the assistant rabbi, Len, who'd let me into his class. I had the corner chair, because nobody else would sit next to me. Half the Seabees had enrolled in the class, including the Rathcart twins, but they couldn't lay a finger on me. Whoever said "Ringworm" was kicked out of class.

Rosemund Rathcart was blonder than Betty Grable, taller and leggier than Rosalind Russell. Even with her eyeglasses, she was almost as beautiful as the dark lady. And when she sketched Launcelot Perry on the blackboard, with pieces of colored chalk— his eyes blue as the Hudson, his cheeks with black hollows, his mouth a little pink—I started to fall in love.

"Class," she said, "chalk is only an instrument, like a rapier or a gun." (I was too ashamed of my ignorance to ask what a rapier was.) "It follows instructions, listens to the mind's eye. The very best artists often draw with their eyes closed."

The class had crayons instead of chalk, and sheets of butcher paper Len had to buy on the black market, and we all attacked the paper with our mind's eye. Mrs. Rathcart asked us to invent a girlfriend for the rat man, a rival to Emma Martins.

I closed my eyes and drew a blond bombshell with glasses and long legs. Mrs. Rathcart studied my drawing and the hat on my head, and whispered to Len. He approached me after class. "I'll have to drop you, Baby. Mrs. Rathcart won't teach with you around. She says you're contagious."

"Not with my hat on, Len, not with the bandages. The

doctor pours tar on my head."

"I'm sorry. It's her class."

I let my misery sink in for a week and then I told mom.

"She's not a dictator," mom said. "You have crayons. Go back to your class."

"Can't, mom. The artist lady won't allow it."

"I'll change her mind."

"Mom, her drawings are in the *Mirror*. She's a big star."

"Baby, I can burn the biggest stars."

I couldn't imagine Faigele as a firebug, but I went back to class with all my crayons. The blond lady was furious. She screamed at Len, called him a coward who couldn't expel one little boy. She stationed me near the window. I couldn't use Len's butcher paper. I had to watch the other kids draw.

Then I heard a knock, and Darcy came wandering into the class with Mr. Lions and a pair of bodyguards clutching fedoras against their hearts. Mom was with them, wearing the lipstick and mascara of a croupier.

It wasn't our borough president who broke the ice. It was Darcy Staples.

"Is it constitutional, Mr. Lions? An art teacher who's also a man of the cloth, discriminating against his own pupils."

"It's undemocratic, to say the least."

"And what if we wrote him a summons? A temple with leaky waterpipes . . . conducting private seminars."

"I have a permit," Len muttered. "A signed document from the mayor's office and the Board of Ed."

"The mayor's office? We don't accept Manhattan mandates. What you need, Lenny boy, is a Bronx seal."

"This is preposterous," said Mrs. Rathcart. "I won't be intimidated. You're gangsters, every single one of you . . . with your own gun moll."

"Gun moll, ma'am?" Darcy said. "This is Mrs. Faigele Charyn, mother of the slandered boy."

Mom smiled like a gorgeous jackal. "The gun moll will burn out your eyes in a minute." And mom lit a match. "Baby, count to three."

But I wouldn't count. Even if Rosemund could draw Launcelot Perry in her mind's eye, I couldn't take the chance.

"I'm a personal friend of the mayor," Rosemund said. "I know the attorney general of the United States."

"Tut," said the dentist. "You'll still need a Bronx seal."

"The boy has ringworm. He shouldn't be here."

"He's not dancing with the other children," mom said. "He's not kissing them, he's not rubbing heads. Do his crayons carry a disease? My son admires you and your pictures. We all admire you. Darcy, have you ever missed an installment of 'Rat Man'?"

"I couldn't live without Launcelot."

"Miles ahead of Dick Tracy and Donald Duck," said our borough president.

I'm not sure if it was flattery or mom's fiery eyes that moved Mrs. Rathcart and rescued me. But I rejoined the class, scribbled on butcher paper. And we celebrated our victory, drank champagne at the Concourse Plaza. Darcy, Mr. Lions, mom, and me. The waiter wasn't supposed to serve alcoholic beverages to a six-year-old. But the Concourse Plaza was Darcy's own canteen, and he insisted that I take a drink.

"To Faigele," Darcy said, "and our gentleman artist, who will grow up to be another Rembrandt."

"To say the least," said Mr. Lions, smashing the champagne glass in his fist.

It was meant to be a sign of luck. But I had no luck in '43. Mrs. Rathcart retired from teaching, and Len discontinued his art class rather than search for a Bronx seal. And I returned to the land of zero. With water bombs as my companion.

The Seabees kept stealing my hats; Newt and Val would taunt me all the time. "Ringworm, you killed our art class. Your mom's a gun moll and a tart."

"What's a tart?"

"A greedy piece of cake," said Newt.

"She does poke in the box with all the politicians," said Val.

"What's *poke in the box?*"

They knocked me on the head with their Seabee bats, and nobody stopped them. They were collecting tin cans for Mr. Roosevelt. They'd been to the White House with their mom. They'd had tea with Mrs. Roosevelt, who loved "Rat Man" and kept a picture of Launcelot and Emma Martins in her bureau. And Mrs. Rathcart's own tailor had cut a miniature Navy cape for the twins, a replica of the one that Roosevelt wore whenever he was on a battleship.

"Good night, Ringworm," Val said, while Newt banged my shoulders. "Sweet dreams."

It was the middle of the afternoon, and I was hatless again. A man sidled up to me, clutching a hatbox. He looked like a very elegant tramp. His suit could have come out of Darcy's closet, but the cuffs were frayed, and the pants hadn't been near an ironing board. His shoes were splattered with white paint; he had bits of stubble around his chin. His face was cut with shadows, like Launcelot Perry. The rat man had such a pull on me, I said, "Launcelot, is that you?"

The rat man laughed. Then I saw the white hair under his fedora, and I recognized my mother's erstwhile partner, Chick Eisenstadt, the black marketeer who'd been boarding at Cedars of Lebanon for months. But the hospital had diminished him. He'd lost his flair.

"Baby," he said.

"My name is Ringworm now."

He opened the hatbox, which was stuffed with baseball caps, black market merchandise. He'd gotten a whole shipment of caps, but they were all from the St. Louis Browns, a team that had never been in the World Series. No Bronx kid would ever wear a Brownie cap. The Brownies lived in hell.

The Yanks had to toss away their own tickets when St. Louis was in town.

"Chick," I said, "I couldn't wear a Brownie hat. The cops will arrest me."

"They won't," Chickie said. "I bought this supply for you. The little bastards can steal your caps night and day, and you'll always have another one."

"But who told you I had the ringworm?"

"Dr. Katz. And I knew you'd have trouble keeping a hat on your head. So I looked for a gross of whatever I could get."

Chick took off his own fedora and put on a Brownie cap. And I didn't have the heart to leave him alone like that, the only guy on the Concourse in a Brownie cap. So I dug into the hatbox and sported the colors and the rigid bill of the St. Louis Browns.

We were like two orphans together, Chick and me. People must have thought we'd escaped from a lunatic asylum in our billed caps. Chick no longer had much of a station at Bitter Eagles. Mom met all of Chickie's old camels at the dentist's office. She couldn't seem to forgive him for letting his wife break in on us at Cedars of Lebanon. It wasn't Chick's fault that Marsha Eisenstadt called me a dope. But the dark lady was a bit like dad. She just didn't have a forgiving nature.

Chick had become his own camel. He carried what he had to carry—in a hatbox or under his shirt. And he doubled as a house painter to make ends meet. He had expensive children, an expensive wife. He painted apartments along the Concourse, working in a Brownie cap and suits that had begun to rot on his back.

Sometimes Chick would take me along on one of his jobs. We would eat sandwiches under the stepladder, listen to the radio, gulp Russian tea out of a huge, insulated bottle. Chick liked to paint with a very fat brush. He would reach across the ladder and cover the length of a wall with a creamy white that left big spots on my cap. He'd let me paint in the corner with a tiny brush that could do little harm. Then he'd laugh and touch up my strokes. He worked very fast. And soon both of us were covered with the same white spots.

He was like a mom and a dad to me, and I wondered what would have happened if Chick had married the dark lady rather than the holy terror of William Howard Taft. Would he have taken his own son on stepladder picnics inside a world of benzene and plaster dust? It was a dangerous business to start reinventing one of your own parents and give yourself a whole new set of ancestors. A tribe of Paley Charyns was bad enough.

Chickie was my big secret. I couldn't tell mom that I'd started a new kind of painting class. But no matter how hard Chick rubbed our clothes with turpentine, we were still two spotted people. And mom began to notice my spots.

"Baby," she said, "are you turning into a leopard or a giraffe?"

"Both," I said, because I didn't know what to say. "Mom, the clouds are getting so fat, it's raining milk in the Bronx."

The next time I went painting with Chick, I started to climb the ladder with him, so we could work in tandem, make the whole planet a creamy white. I discovered a guest under our ladder. The dark lady in her card dealer's clothes. She saw the paint in our eyes. "My two bitter eagles," she said, "who like to fly near the ceiling."

We came down off the ladder. Chick with his brush, me with mine. Mom began to scold him. "Mr. Eisenstadt, didn't you ever hear of the child labor laws?"

Mom's ex-partner was mortified. "Faigele, did I lose my name in the street? I'm Chick."

"The Chick I remember wouldn't take advantage of a boy with ringworm."

"Mom, he didn't," I said. "Chick got me ten dozen baseball caps so I wouldn't have to go around bald."

"Better bald," mom said, "than dust in your lungs to catch tuberculosis. A boy needs fresh air."

"Faigele, the fresh air was costing him."

"Fresh air is free."

"Not when other boys hit him and steal his hats."

"I'm no sissy," mom said. "I'll fight those boys."

"Half the Bronx?"

"Then I'll hire the other half to fight the half that steals his hats."

And mom stole me away from Uncle Chick, dragged me out of there with my spotted cap.

Desert Boy

I had a whole colony of hats, a leaning tower devoted to the St. Louis Browns. And I was the little mad hatter who marched in the streets. But I missed that other dad of mine, Uncle Chick. I'd fallen in love with the smell of turpentine and with the white spots on my shoes. I'd had a job, after all, as Chick's apprentice, and I didn't dream of school while I mounted the ladder or ate sandwiches with Chick. I would have been happy to be a house painter, as long as Chick was beside me, listening to the radio. But I didn't have Chick, and I turned melancholic when the school year started without me. I had my crayons and my bottle of glue, but I couldn't venture into P.S. 88, a converted firehouse at the top of the hill, a hundred years old, with dark red walls. I had to watch while every single kid near the Concourse converged on *my* school with their pencil cases.

My heart was like a bitter ball. I had so much malice inside me, I could have burnt the school down if someone had put a match in my hand. But I should have been glad. No one shouted "Ringworm" or stole my hat during school hours, when the Seabees were tucked inside that ancient firehouse, and I was free to roam wherever I wanted. I would visit the soldier who was stationed in Claremont Park. He had nothing to do but sit in the tiny saddle of an antiaircraft gun that was pointed at the blue skies of the Bronx. I'm not even sure this ack-ack gun had any shells. But the soldier sat. He would lower and raise the saddle with the same little lever that Darcy had on his dentist's chair. And he wore a white helmet, like my dad. We were both outcasts, him with his crazy cannon, me with my poisoned scalp, and I had a touch of affection for such a soldier with his unfriendly, crooked face and a cigarette hanging from his chapped lips. He flirted with the housewives who trundled their baby carriages past his little domain, but none of them cared about a simple soldier with an ack-ack gun. He was always alone.

He would ride up and down on his saddle, rotate the gun, pretend he was knocking a German bomber out of the sky, but there was nothing to shoot at, not even a sparrow, a pigeon, or a kite. He was a prisoner of the people, condemned to take part in a ludicrous vigil.

The Seabees loathed him, because he wasn't with the Navy. They would arrive after school, hurl stones at him, taunt him from some distant rock, and if I waited around too long, they would come after me, grab my hat, rub my face in the grass.

The soldier never climbed down from his saddle to rescue me. He had to protect the skies. But once, in early October, while the Rathcart twins and five other Seabees had trapped me in Claremont Park and were punching me with their usual vigor, a powerful wind seemed to sweep off the rocks and slap them into the ground right in the middle of their war chant. "Ringworm, Ringworm." That wind had brown eyes and my mother's swarthy look.

All seven Seabees began to blubber and shout. "We didn't mean it, Harve. We won't touch Ringworm again."

"What's Ringworm's regular name?"

"Baby, Baby Charyn," sang Val and Newt, and they ran out of the park with their miserable pack of Seabees. I was left with my brother Harvey, nine years old, who suffered from asthma. He didn't get along with mom. She'd sentenced him to a school for asthmatics in the desert, at Tucson, Arizona. But the dark lady wasn't being cruel. Harve couldn't breathe the Bronx's wet air. The desert had saved his life.

His skin was much darker than mine, and he was as lanky as a snake. I hadn't seen Harve in twelve or thirteen months.

He'd gotten rid of the Rathcarts, but he wouldn't hug me or say hello. He scooped me out of the grass and began to kick me across Claremont Park. They weren't his hardest kicks, but they still hurt.

"You've been ganging up against dad, you and mom."

"Harve, I swear, I took dad to his shop. He doesn't need me anymore. You can ask him yourself."

"I don't have to ask. Mom is never home. Dad has to suck dry beans at the fur market."

"Mom can't help it. She's a politician now. She's gonna keep Roosevelt in the White House."

"Don't lie. She's a card dealer. And she runs a branch of the black market."

"It's only a little branch," I said, and Harve kicked me right into the water fountain. I figured it was safer to keep quiet. I took off the baseball hat. Harve always hated the Browns.

"Dunce," he said. "Put your hat on. Nobody has to look at your ringworm."

"But ringworm isn't as rotten as the St. Louis Browns."

He kicked me where my tail began. I had to walk bent over, like an old guy.

"I've been to St. Louis, and it ain't so bad."

"Did you see the Brownies play?"

"It was winter. The Brownies were asleep."

"Then what's so hot about St. Louis?"

"It's America," he said, and I was trying hard to believe him.

"What about us? We have the Concourse and Charlie Keller and more lions than any other zoo."

"That's right," Harve said. "The Bronx is one big lion cage."

"But lions are American too."

Harve was so disgusted, he stopped kicking me. And we walked home, my brother like a Bronx god with Arizona on his face. Dad was upstairs. Harve must have called him at his shop. He danced and started to cry when he saw my brother.

"I missed you, Harvey, missed you very much." But he'd never talked about Harve, never mentioned him all the time Harvey was away. Was it the dark lady's doing? Did mom have some power over dad? And what about little Ringworm? I was the one who picked up Harvey's postcards from the mailbox, delivered them to mom and dad, but none of us could read his handwriting. And I can't recall mom ever showing the cards to Chick. They were Harvey's personal hieroglyphics. Mom took the cards, kept them in the same wooden chest with all her letters from Mogilev. Once or twice I caught her looking at the cards late at night, trying to decipher Harvey's scrawl. But the moment she saw me, mom threw them back inside the chest. Harvey's language was between him and her.

Dad took Harve and me to have an early dinner at Bitter Eagles. We sat near all the Tatar gangsters, who had Harve's Mongolian eyes. The gangsters gave us vodka to drink. They must have felt a certain kinship with my brother that went beyond the shape and color of his eyes.

"Sonny," they said. "We haven't seen you. Where are you from?"

"I live in Arizona," Harve said.

"Do you happen to know Blackie Shamberg? He moved to Phoenix five years ago."

"I'm from Tucson."

"That's a shame," the gangsters said. "Blackie would have enjoyed you. You're his type."

These Tatars wouldn't let us pay for our meal. They offered each of us a dessert and drank Mongolian tea at our table. They all wore gold bracelets and pinkie rings and chains around their necks. They dressed like parakeets, in yellow green and powder blue.

Harvey told them his name.

"Ah, Faigele's kid . . . It's curious. You have a head of hair, and Faigele's kid is supposed to be bald."

"That's my brother, Baby Jerome."

"Him with the funny cap? Then Faigele has a whole team of boys. But tell her to be careful. Her dentist is about to take a fall."

"What dentist?" Harvey had to ask.

"There's only one. Darcy Staples. And the governor has singled him out. Tom Dewey is declaring war on the Bronx."

Dewey wanted to run against Roosevelt in 1944. He was the Republicans' own dark horse. Dewey beat up all the downtown gangsters when he was Manhattan's district attorney, sent them to jail. And now he was attacking Roosevelt's people in the Bronx. Boss Flynn liked to call him that lousy kid with the mustache. Dewey wasn't really a kid. He was forty-one, but he'd still be the youngest President we ever had, if he could knock FDR out of the White House.

It was dad's misfortune to have the same kind of mustache as Tom Dewey. The gangsters grew suspicious.

"Is he a friend of yours?" they asked Harve.

"That's my dad, Sergeant Sam."

"Ah, the air-raid warden." They shook dad's hand. "Congratulations. You have a terrific tribe."

The gangsters insisted on driving us home in their personal taxicab. We arrived around midnight, a few minutes before Mom. Her hair was swept back like a movie star. Her lips were a gorgeous red gash. She was coming from a soiree at the Concourse Plaza. She wore her silver fox, a scarlet dress, and purple shoes. She wobbled into the apartment with champagne fever in her eyes. But the fever disappeared when she saw Harve. "The desert boy," she muttered. "Couldn't you warn us when you were coming home?"

And that lanky snake lost his swagger. "I did, mom. In my last postcard."

"Who can read your cards?" she said. "Who can read your cards?"

The dark lady took my brother in her arms, held him

against the silver fox for a long time.

"Mom," I said, "Darcy's in a whole lot of trouble."

"Who told you that?"

"A coupla crooks at Bitter Eagles."

"You went to *my* restaurant without me?"

"Mom," I said, "we had to eat."

"And what did the bandits have to say?"

"That Dewey's gonna bring down the Bronx."

That red wound opened wide, and the dark lady let out a laugh. "Dewey can't touch us. The dentist will eat him alive . . . Harvey, do I have to search for your postcards? Why are you here?"

"The Sea Scouts are having a parade. I didn't want to miss it."

"You ran all the way from Arizona for one little parade?"

"I had to, mom. I couldn't desert my crew."

Harve was one of the first Sea Scouts in the Bronx. The Scouts were junior cadets that the Navy began to organize and encourage in case the war didn't end and the country ran out of sailors. Boss Flynn and FDR had blessed the Bronx's own fleet of Scouts.

"And how will you get back to Arizona?"

"I'll hitch," Harve said.

"No one in my family will start thumbing rides. Sam, talk to him. Insist."

"Mom, it never fails. I wear my uniform. I look just like a sailor. Everybody stops for me."

"Sam, I'll kill him," the dark lady screamed, and we fed her hot milk. All of us had the hiccups, even dad. Mom kissed Harve good night. "My gangster," she said, "my Sea Scout."

Mom and dad went off to their bed, and Harve and me to mine. I loved to sleep with Harve in the same bed. He'd brought a magic gun with him from Arizona. The gun had a bulb near the trigger, and it could shoot pictures on a dark wall. We watched naked women for half an hour. Their bodies

jiggled. They weren't beautiful, not like Joan Crawford . . . or
Faigele. They had wandering pink eyes, like crazed barracudas
that couldn't seem to look into the light. And I wondered if
these were the same wild women dad had met in Miami, only
they weren't so wild, and what was Harvey doing with their
images in his lantern gun?

"Hot stuff, huh, Baby?"

I was disappointed, but I didn't tell Harve. I would have
preferred pictures of Tucson coming out of that gun. Where
was that America Harve had been bragging about? I shut my
eyes and fell asleep while a naked dancer rolled her belly on
the wall.

The world was different with Harvey around. No one called
me Ringworm. No one tried to steal my hat. The Seabees would
have murdered anyone who bothered Baby. My brother wasn't a
prince, like Darcy Staples. He didn't have his own dentist's chair,
or a gang of hoodlum cops, but he couldn't get away from
politics. The Rathcart twins groveled around him. They could
call themselves Seabees, but they weren't real Scouts, and they
were hoping Harve had some pull and could help them march
in the parade. But what kind of parade would it have been if
Harve had to march with Newt and Val?

Maybe he was a prince. Mom let him lie in bed as long as he
liked, and she started squeezing oranges for Harve; asthmatics couldn't live without orange juice. And Harve was the only
one in the house who could scribble a note to the telephone
company, even if his handwriting wasn't terrific. He'd perfect-
ed his English in Arizona, solved all the riddles of grammar
that ruined mom and me. He laughed at our little reading lessons, said *Bambi* was for infants. He'd gone through the library
at Tucson, talked of Jack London and Huckleberry Finn, a man
in an iron mask, and a monster called Mr. Hyde. Dad wasn't
interested in monsters and tramps, but I looked at Faigele, and
Faigele looked at me. Neither of us could recover from all the

characters Harvey had ripped out of those library books and stored inside his head. We loved Harve, but I understood why mom had exiled him. Asthma was only an excuse. We would have eaten our hearts out wanting to be like my brother.

He was dad's champion, went with him to the fur market, had lunch with dad and his boss. But dad could afford to love Harve without limits. Dad wasn't a reader. Jack London and George Sand meant nothing to him. He had no use for wild dogs and men in iron masks. He could only measure things with the mark of his knife.

The dark lady was cautious around my brother. She took him to meet the dentist, had him sit with her at a card game. Darcy was in a charitable mood; he let my brother have a hand in the game. No other nine-year-old had ever held cards at Darcy's table. Harve bluffed the police captains, the Bronx senators, and Mr. Lions, and walked away with fifty dollars, but he wouldn't warm to the dentist or acknowledge the gift Darcy had given him: a seat at the poker table.

"What's that?" my brother asked, pointing to an empty chair. "Is it reserved for Roosevelt?"

"No," Mr. Lions said. "But it's the nearest thing. The chief sits there whenever he's in town. Old Flynn."

"That's funny," Harve said with a cat's smile. "I thought it was Governor Dewey's chair."

"God forbid."

The gamblers stared at Darcy, who stroked his silver mustache.

"Boss, should I beat his ears back?" said one of the hoodlum cops. "Faigele's son can't insult us . . . not after we let him win."

"The boy has pluck," Darcy said, "and shut your mouth. Faigele runs a fair game."

"Harve didn't mean anything," I said. "We heard a rumor at the Russian restaurant. Roosevelt locked Dewey out of the Bronx, and Dewey is gonna take revenge. But he can't touch this card game, can he, Mr. Lions?"

"Not unless he wants to lose his own head of hair. Tom Dewey'll never walk through this door while I'm president of the Bronx."

"He'll walk where he has to walk," Darcy said. Then he turned to my brother and shut Mr. Lions out of his mind.

"Faigele says you're the reader in the family. Devoted to Mr. Jack London. I loved *Call of the Wild* when I was a lad. And Mr. Stevenson's books. But I don't believe in Dr. Jekyll or Mr. Hyde."

Harve shoved the fifty dollars into his shirt. "What do you believe in?"

"Literature, and not tales of a grim boy like Mr. Hyde. You won't find that silly stuff in Chekhov."

"What did he write?" I had to ask.

"Masterpieces," Darcy said, and he rattled off titles as if they were liquid flavors at a soda fountain. *"The Seagull, The Seven Sisters, The Dark Lady with the Little Dog"*

"Uncle Darcy," I said, jumping up and down, "tell me about that dark lady and her dog."

"He's not your uncle," Harve said, "and I never heard of Chekhov. There are no Chekhovs at the Tucson library, or I would have noticed his name."

"Indeed," Darcy said. "Then Tucson is in a very bad state . . . Faigele, will you enlighten this desert rat, inform him of Chekhov's literary repute."

"Darcy," mom said, "your Mr. Chekhov escapes me."

"But he was born in Belorusse, if I remember, minutes from your door. You must have studied him at school."

"School," Mom said, "what school? I was running from the tzar *and* the Revolution. I didn't have time for dark ladies and their little dogs, or any other masterpieces."

"Her name is Anna. She's a divorcee who's come to Nice. She can't afford to stay at any of the grand palaces on the beach.

She has to live at a tiny boardinghouse near the boulevard du Tzarewitch."

"What's a tzarewitch?"

"Don't interrupt," Darcy said. "A tzarewitch is the son of a tzar, his principal heir, but this Anna had no heirs, only a dog whose name was Dog. That's how desperate she was. She couldn't dream up the dog's own individual name. She fell in love with a gigolo who was living closer to the beach. He sucked out whatever little money she had, abandoned her, and Anna decides to drown herself and her dog in the bay. Poor Anna succeeds, but the dog has a much stronger constitution than his mistress, swims back to shore, and is immediately adopted by the gigolo, who employs this dog named Dog to help him seduce other women."

"A masterpiece," said Mr. Lions, bawling into his handkerchief. "The gigolo should have been shot . . . with the dog."

"But that's the beauty of it," Darcy said. "Chekhov doesn't condemn his own people . . . that's why they continue to haunt us. Wouldn't you agree, Mr. Harvey Charyn?"

Harve returned the fifty dollars to the table and walked out of the dentist's retreat. Mom didn't mention Darcy to him again. And Harve joined other Sea Scouts at the Kingsbridge Armory to prepare for the parade. Meanwhile, Mrs. Daniel Kaplan, whose son George had been killed aboard a battleship, lost the red banner in her window with the gold star that was meant to honor George. Somebody had plucked the banner right out of the window. Darcy offered a thousand dollars to anyone who could recapture the gold star. His own police captains couldn't come up with any clues. But I remembered those air-raid wardens who carried enormous sacks on their shoulders the night I followed dad into the Church—his headquarters on Sheridan Avenue. I couldn't ask dad if his brother wardens were thieves; I told Harve, who broke into the Church, discovered Mrs. Kaplan's banner behind a bin,

and gave it to mom. Mom called Darcy, and he arrived at
the Church with a police captain, looked at all the stolen merchandise, assembled the two guilty wardens and the dispatcher
with chubby fingers who smoked cigars like a man. No one
arrested them. That would have been a black mark against
the Bronx. The dentist simply held his own court inside the
Church, punched and kicked the fat dispatcher and her two
accomplices, who were going to sell Mrs. Kaplan's gold star to
some miserable collector of wartime memorabilia. He locked
the Church, shut it down forever, returned the gold star to
Mrs. Kaplan, and wrote a check to Harvey Charyn for a thousand dollars. But my brother threw it right back at the dentist.

"Give it to the Red Cross," he said.

Mr. Lions was there, and he was furious. "What kind of boy
doesn't want pocket money?"

"This kind of boy," Harve said, and Darcy tore up the check.
But it was dad who suffered the most. He lost his sergeant's station. Darcy wouldn't allow *any* wardens to patrol his terrain.
Dad couldn't go into the street with his helmet strapped on
and make his usual rounds. Air-raid wardens had become pa-
riahs, peddlers of sacred articles. Darcy wouldn't dare accuse
dad of the crime, but dad was still tainted. The dark lady kept
clawing at him. "You must have known what this Miriam was
doing. You have eyes. Didn't you see Mrs. Kaplan's gold star?"

"The Church was dark," dad said.

"You had a flashlight, Sergeant Sam."

"I had to preserve my batteries for the street."

"Faker," mom said. "How much did that fat whore pay you
to keep quiet?"

"I never took her merchandise. I never stole. I had nothing
to do with the black market."

"Sweet man," mom said, "you looked for every airplane in
the sky . . . and the rottenness was all around you."

They slapped each other, and my brother had to get between them. "Mom, leave him alone. He's the best air-raid warden in the Bronx."

"The best retired warden, my dear. Can I show my face to Mrs. Kaplan and the other mothers with dead sons?"

"Mom, dad didn't do a thing."

"That's the story in a nutshell. Didn't do a thing, when he could have reported those lousy burglars."

"He's no cop. And he doesn't have a dentist behind him."

"Darcy's a great man," mom said. "A patriot. He helps the poor, cleans their teeth."

"And their pockets, mom."

"Go on. Slander him. When your father couldn't work, who put food on our table, who gave me a job?"

"Gamblers always know how to pick a pretty face."

"Don't talk that way to your mother," dad said.

"Dad, dad, she's the dentist's bathing beauty."

Dad slapped his own champion. Harve didn't even resist. He took the slap. And then he started to cough. Mom had to boil a big pot of water, pour it into a basin, and have my brother stand with a towel over his head and suck up the steam coming off the basin. Dad shuffled next to him with tears in his eyes. "Harvey, I didn't mean the slap—"

"Sam," my mother shouted, "stop it. He'll choke if he gets excited."

Harve had to stay in bed. He looked like a prisoner in his pajamas. He lived near steam basins and mustard plasters, bottles of medicine and sprays. Mom said his lungs would turn to paper if he didn't sleep with mustard on his chest. Meyer Lansky's doctor came to the house and examined Harve. He told mom to get rid of all her mustard plasters. "Faigele, it's wet air. That's the killer. Send him back to Arizona."

"Doctor, he's a boy, not a postage stamp. I can't send him through the mail."

My brother started to wheeze; it was the asthmatics' whistle, and that's why Harve's enemies in the Bronx called him the Whistler. His lips turned blue. Dr. Katz went into his medical kit, pulled out a dark cigarette that was a foot long. He lit that long cigarette, and made my brother breathe the fumes.

I nearly died. That's how awful the stink was—like the acid coming off a dozen rotting rats. But the wheezing stopped, and Harve's lips regained their natural color. The doctor let my mother have two "sulphur cigarettes." He borrowed mom's vacuum cleaner and started to dust the ceiling and the walls, the mattress and the pillowcases, with a lyrical sweep of his arms and legs.

"Doctor," mom said, "I would never have guessed you did housecleaning on the side."

"It's nothing. I do it for Lansky all the time. He's allergic to dust."

"Will there be dust on the Grand Concourse when my son marches in the big parade?"

"Darling," the doctor said, "you'll have to stand behind him with a broom and a gas mask."

"They'll think he's a mama's boy"

"Mom," I said, "you could cut your hair and dress up like a Sea Scout."

The doctor blinked at my mother. "Baby, it wouldn't work." Then he plucked off my baseball cap and peeked at my scalp.

"When can I go to school?"

"Soon," he said, and ran out the door. He wouldn't accept payment from us. We were Darcy's people. We belonged to the dentist.

Harve hated being an invalid. Mom wouldn't let him go near the armory without me. I was his nurse. I carried the sulphur cigarettes and a bunch of matches in one of Faigele's own shoeboxes. I sat in the stands with other guests while Harve marched downstairs in the main hall. He wore white spats and a webbed belt, a would-be sailor in a little sea of sailors; maybe his shoes weren't properly shined, and none of his nails was a perfect half-moon, but isn't that how Launcelot Perry would have behaved, if the rat man had ever been a Scout?

Harve was smaller than the other Scouts, who were eleven and twelve, and had slept one night on a Coast Guard cutter called *The Courage*. They marched with a certain swagger, but it was mostly a bluff; they didn't have that inward turn of the eye, like the rat man and my brother, a sense of isolation that could only have come from living in a boxcar or behind a garbage barrel ...

Boss Flynn was grand marshal of the parade. He rode in a Cadillac with Darcy and Mr. Lions, in front of all the Scouts. He was either the biggest, roundest man I'd ever seen, or else it was an optical illusion, with the sun poisoning my eye. He had six chins, and a rose in his lapel that looked like a fistful of blood. He clutched a microphone and kept evoking the President's name. "Franklin Roosevelt . . . how that man loves a parade. 'Ed,' he told me, 'I'm proud of your marching boys, your boys of the Bronx.'"

Mom and dad were at the parade, and dad cried when he saw Harve march in the middle of a swollen file, vulnerable to all the dust in the trees, his lips potentially blue, his lungs ready to rip. But Baby wouldn't cry. I cursed the parade. Mrs. Roosevelt must have put some pressure on Boss Flynn, because he let Newt and Val into the Scouts at the last minute, and my brother had to march with the Rathcart twins, who stumbled in their spats, and broke the Scouts' gorgeous white line.

Harve returned to bed after the parade. We had to endure the intolerable stink of a sulphur cigarette, but Harve recovered a little after he breathed the fumes. It was Darcy who rescued him, found my brother a berth on a military train that was passing through Arizona. We went to the station with Harve. I watched Faigele's eyes begin to flutter. She was about to swoon. She hated Harve, and couldn't bear to see him go. It was Darcy who caught my mother, not dad. He'd arrived at Pennsylvania Station in a cream-colored coat, with a copy of *Jekyll and Hyde* bound in morocco, Harve's initials burnt right into the leather skin.

I think I understand the dentist; he liked me a lot, but he admired Harve, the Whistler who wouldn't take a thousand-dollar reward.

We waved to Harve. He'd never even talked about his school in Arizona, or his loneliness without the Bronx; America was his new mom and dad.

Faigele fell into a black hole; she was too weak to wash her own hair. I had to cook for her, encourage dad to drink his schnapps. Baby had become the little man of the house. I missed Harve. He was my hero. But I could console myself with the rat man, follow his adventures every week. And mom began to climb out of her funk.

"He's better off, isn't he, Baby?"

"Harve has the sun."

"You'll start school, we'll learn how to write, and we'll get closer to Harvey."

"Mom," I said, "even if I went to college, I couldn't read Harve's handwriting. Nobody can."

"Don't lie," she said. "We'll learn."

Mom stood in the mirror, combed her hair, painted her mouth with the luminous red eye of her lipstick, and went down to deal cards for the dentist.

Madame Curie

Her married name was Madame Curie. But she was born Maria Sklodowska in Warsaw, in 1867. Her dad was a lowly teacher of mathematics who lost his money gambling on the stock exchange, and Maria was an infant prodigy who could memorize maps and countries and languages before she was five. She went to the Russian lycée, where she wore out her professors with her knowledge of Spinoza and the laws of physics. But she couldn't attend the university because of her father's misfortune. Maria, the most brilliant girl in her class, became a governess at seventeen. Her mind fell asleep. She lived like a dray horse to support her family. Finally she fled to Paris, continued her studies at the Sorbonne. She fell in love with a French scientist, Pierre Curie, married him, worked in his lab. They discovered radium together, shared the Nobel prize in 1903. But in 1906 Pierre was run over by a dray on the rue Dauphine and died on the spot. Madame Curie went on with their experiments in radioactivity, and was the first woman to ever teach at the Sorbonne. She won a second Nobel prize in 1911. The most celebrated person on the planet, more popular than movie stars and kings, she sacrificed herself to science. The radioactive material in her lab began to poison Madame Curie; her blood turned to water, and she died of leukemia in 1934.

MGM decided to cash in on her life, and produced *Madame Curie,* the biggest blockbuster of 1943, starring Greer Garson, a redhead who didn't really look like Faigele. But she played a dark lady in the film. The whole Bronx fell in love with MGM's Madame Curie. Greer Garson was in the window of every shop; she never posed as a bathing beauty. She was the

Bronx's hysterical idea of the perfect woman, a gorgeous widow who wastes away in a laboratory. And because Poland was considered next door to Belorusse, and Greer Garson was much more radiant than all the men around her, Darcy and his tribe of politicians began to call my mother Madame Curie.

"Faigele," Mr. Lions said, "you should have married a physicist."

"How could I have flirted with him, Mr. Lions? There are no Russian lycées in the Bronx."

But I could tell that MGM had moved mom; she must have wondered what it would have been like to live in a world of scientists, where she might have discovered some radioactive material to combat ringworm. Faigele had long-range plans. She'd wait until I finished junior high, and we'd go to high school together, Madame Curie & Son at William Howard Taft. But I couldn't even manage first grade. The sores healed on my head, and I arrived at P.S. 88 one morning in early December with my crayons and pencil case. I still had a couple of bald spots, and everybody, including my teacher, was suspicious. I wore my Brownie cap and sat at a special desk, far from my classmates. I couldn't hear a thing. I was like a shell-shocked boy, an invalid who could only pick up pieces of language.

The school sent me to a hearing clinic in the winter of '44. I rode down to the clinic with Madame Curie and Mr. Lions. I wore earphones for an hour, listened to very strange bells: the silence between the bells was like a separate civilization, where music was outlawed, and nothing could ever begin or end. I thought of that cantor, Gilbert Rogovin, during the silence between the bells, when I realized that you couldn't live without a melody. Our miserable cantor had nourished a whole synagogue with his songs. I missed the chanting he did in his white hat. But I survived, and the clinic told my mother that I wasn't deaf.

I should have been glad, but I couldn't rejoice with mom

and Mr. Lions. "Madame Curie," whispered the president of the Bronx. "Madame Curie." He kept purring in mom's ear. He brought us to the dentist, but Darcy's building was flooded with cops. They stole his files, stored in a hundred shoeboxes, and stuffed them into a police wagon. It wasn't the Bronx police. Tom Dewey sent a special prosecutor down on Darcy, and the prosecutor had his own police from Manhattan.

"Put back the shoeboxes," Mr. Lions screamed. He summoned several Bronx police captains, but they couldn't do a thing. Darcy had already been arrested. He languished in Manhattan's criminal court, like the man in the iron mask. Fifty Democrats arrived at the arraignment, citizens of the Bronx who put up Darcy's bail and carried him from the courthouse on their shoulders, shouting "Tom Dewey can't soil our prince."

Mr. Lions wanted to declare a holiday in the Bronx, but the dentist said no. "Let's not draw attention to ourselves." His silver mustache didn't seem so silver. He must have frozen in Manhattan. He kept warming his hands in his own pockets. Dewey was calling him a swindler and a black marketeer. Mr. Lions arranged a party at the Concourse Plaza to raise some cash for Darcy's defense fund. The Bronx police captains were there and all the politicians, except Boss Flynn. Mr. Lions didn't even have a telegram from Roosevelt to read. The White House was suddenly neutral in the war between Tom Dewey and the Bronx.

Mr. Lions had invited an impresario to sing. Gilbert Rogovin arrived from the Cincinnati Opera House. He was much fatter than I remembered him to be. Rogovin wouldn't do any of his synagogue songs. He did Don Giovanni. He couldn't take his eyes off Faigele. She wore a red dress that was like a victory banner. The cantor shivered when he played the Barber of Seville. He shoved ten dollars into my fist. "Tell Faigele I have a room on the third floor. I'll die if she doesn't visit me."

I took his money but I wouldn't deliver the message. He drank half a bottle of whisky and collapsed in his chair, under a thick mask of paint that made him look like a tired clown.

Darcy kept waiting for a telephone call from his chief, a few words that would redeem him and his struggle. But Boss Flynn never called. And Darcy did something foolish. He broke the terms of his bail. He wasn't supposed to leave the Bronx without a permit from the special prosecutor. It was a plot to embarrass Darcy, keep him hemmed in. But he ran to Jersey City to visit a whore and collect a bill, and Dewey's detectives tracked him down and brought him to the Tombs. It was slightly illegal, but they seemed to have warrants that allowed them to cross the Hudson and kidnap Darcy, remove him from his favorite brothel. He could have had another bail hearing, but he decided to rot in the Tombs. The prince of the Grand Concourse chose to live in exile if Boss Flynn couldn't punish Tom Dewey and stop his commando raids on the Bronx.

We visited Darcy at the Tombs. It was Manhattan's own penitentiary, meant for the hardest cases. The dentist had to live around criminals all day. The Tombs was like a huge, abandoned tugboat that was sinking into the ground. It had no windows that I could see, and even if it did, Darcy was still deprived of the precious winter light that floated off the roofs of the Concourse near sundown. He had his own cell, with an armchair and a radio and a little electric coffeepot that Darcy claimed was standard gear for "political prisoners." Mom had baked him some Russian coffee cake, and the dentist closed his eyes when he tasted the dark chocolate.

"It's a dream," he said, and I almost cried, because Darcy had been the best-dressed man in the Bronx, and now he wore the ragged gray uniform of a jailbird. He wouldn't ask his tailor, Feuerman & Marx, to travel downtown and fit him with custom-made prison clothes. And he wouldn't trim his mustache while he was in the Tombs; silver hair wandered all over his face. But the Russian cake had revived him.

He looked into Faigele's eyes. "Has Lions kept you on the payroll? You get your usual cut, whether there's a card game or not."

But there was no payroll; Darcy's assets, visible and invisible, had disappeared with the hundred shoeboxes and his dentist's chair.

"I love you both," he said, grabbing my hand and smiling at Faigele, with bits of dark chocolate between his teeth.

"Baby," he said, "I'll send you to law school ... we'll need a lawyer like you. The President has abandoned us. I've been breaking heads fifteen years for that man in the White House. We stole the vote for him when he ran for governor. Mr. Frank couldn't win without Syracuse, and we delivered Syracuse, in a barrel of blood . . . Baby, will you go to law school?"

"I promise."

"Ah, I'm content," Darcy said. "I can sleep, knowing that we have a future."

But the dentist had no future. He died of a heart attack in his cell. He was forty-one years old, like Tom Dewey. Mr. Lions had to create a burial fund for him. Darcy wanted to lie near Herman Melville in Woodlawn, the Bronx's own cemetery. Mr. Lions was in a panic. Nobody had ever heard of Melville.

"Mr. Lions," I said, "he must be related to Chekhov. Darcy loved Chekhov."

"Who's Chekhov?"

"A writer."

"Why didn't you say so?"

And he looked up Herman Melville in the Bronx almanac. Melville was a composer of sea stories, and a sailor who lived with cannibals in Tahiti, the almanac said. "His classic, *Moby Dick; or The Whale*, was largely unread in his lifetime." He stopped writing novels altogether when he was thirty-six, became a forgotten man, with a very long beard. "Herman was rescued from Manhattan's vapors and laid to rest in Woodlawn, among the flowers."

Mr. Lions buried Darcy as close to Herman Melville as he could. The cemetery was very crowded. It sat on a hill, and Darcy couldn't have seen Melville's grave from his own plot. A platoon of politicians appeared at the burial. Boss Flynn had come with his people. He kept blowing his nose into the largest handkerchief I ever saw. "A tragedy," he said. "One of our better sons."

Mom wore a veil on that hill, like Darcy's other "widows." She didn't cry, but I know how sad she was. She'd discovered the English language around Darcy Staples, had crawled out of her immigrant's shell to deal cards and meet the president of the Bronx and other bigwigs.

There were no priests or rabbis running around. Darcy was a Protestant, and maybe that's why Boss Flynn had sacrificed him so fast. Protestants were like outlaws in the Bronx. FDR was a Protestant, but nobody held it against him, because he was from Hyde Park, where all the Protestants lived. But he couldn't have been elected president of the Bronx, like Mr. Lions . . .

One of the mourners seemed familiar in his brown derby. His mustache had darkened in the past six months, but he didn't have any spots on his shoes. It was Uncle Chick, the house painter, who'd prospered away from Bitter Eagles. He'd gone into business with one of Meyer Lansky's lieutenants, and now he was a contractor who supervised the painting of apartment houses and hospitals and parochial schools.

"Faigele," he said, "am I forgiven?"

Faigele was like a sphinx under her veil. "Mr. Eisenstadt," she said, "I liked you better with paint on your shoes."

"That's funny. You gave the opposite impression."

"Why are you here? To pursue me and my son in a cemetery?"

"No. To pay my respects to a dead man."

"Darcy hated you. His cowboys put you in the hospital . . . you still haven't healed."

"He was a warrior. Under the circumstances, I would have done the same to him."

"What circumstances?"

"He was in love with you."

"That's news," Faigele said. "He lived in a bordello."

"He was in love with you. You're the only woman he would have ever married."

"Who told you that?"

"The dentist. He admitted it to me. That's why he had to break my head."

"Men have such wonderful logic."

Mom lifted her veil with one finger. The dark lady was blushing in that cemetery of flowers, where Darcy slept on the same hill with Herman Melville, author of *The Whale.* "How's your missus?"

"We're estranged," Chickie said.

I clucked in Faigele's ear: if she went to William Howard Taft, mom would have to get along with Marsha Eisenstadt, who might become the assistant principal in seven or eight years.

"House painter," mom said, "don't neglect your children," and she waltzed me away from Chick.

Mr. Lions began courting mom a week after the burial. He came knocking at our door with a whole plantation of roses that hid half his head. He wanted to install mom at the Concourse Plaza with her own card game. "We have Flynn's blessing. The Boss is taken with you. He said, 'Faigele ought to climb into our coach. And she can bring aboard that little boy with ringworm.'"

"Baby doesn't have ringworm anymore. Haven't you noticed, Mr. Lions? And why are you sucking up to the man who sentenced Darcy to death?"

"God forbid," said Mr. Lions. "The dentist died of heart failure."

"Heartbreak is a better word. He was a political prisoner."

"Faigele, it's an election year. FDR couldn't afford a brouhaha in the Bronx. He had to give Dewey a little bone. Flynn's hands were tied."

"A little bone? Then you can play cards with Flynn and every other boss whose hands are tied."

"Faigele, it's politics. Darcy was my friend."

Mom returned the plantation of roses and said good-bye to the president of the Bronx. She took FDR's picture off the wall. Sergeant Sam nearly choked on his schnapps.

"Faigele, he's President of the United States."

"Not in my house."

Mom had abandoned all her prospects. She no longer had money to burn. I couldn't go into a toy shop, shut my eyes, and pick out some bagatelle, like a pirate pistol or a statuette of Bambi. I liked it better when mom was in the black market.

I would sneak out of school whenever Chick invited mom to lunch at Bitter Eagles. The restaurant had to take him back. The Russian gangsters who huddled near the bar couldn't afford to slap Meyer Lansky in the face. Chick was attached to Lansky's own lieutenant. None of the gangsters had ever seen Meyer, who lived on Central Park West, but they didn't want to tangle with the Little Man. He was the childhood friend of Bugsy Siegel, psychopath and founder of Las Vegas; a disciple of Arnold Rothstein, first tzar of organized crime; a partner of Lucky Luciano, Rothstein's own little tzarewitch. But Meyer had managed to keep his photograph out of the American papers; there were no features about the Little Man, except in the Jewish press, which talked of his donations to synagogues and summer camps. But the Bronx, *and* Bitter Eagles, seemed to know more about Meyer than the Manhattan district attorney and the *New York Times.* Philanthropic gambler, jukebox king,

loyal Democrat, he shunned publicity. The Russian gangsters
wanted to know if Chick had met the Little Man.

"What's he like? Chickie, does he have cold eyes?"

"Gentlemen, he's as endearing as Santa Claus. Mind, I only
met with him for five minutes. He asked how the Bronx could
survive without Joe DiMaggio."

"Did Meyer lose his head in the sand? DiMaggio's fighting
for America. He doesn't have time for baseball . . . "

"Then you tell that to the Little Man."

The Russian gangsters dug their noses into their vodka glasses.
And Chick invited mom and me on a tour of his domain.
I watched two hundred painters descend upon a hospital and
whiten every wall in half a day. Chickie called it the shock treatment, because no one could match the discipline and the
speed of his house painters. He'd underbid all other contractors in the Bronx, and he had to "deliver" a hospital in an
impossibly short period, or waive his fee. He would move his
arms like an orchestra leader—Chick had his own baton—
and tap any of his shock troops who fell asleep on the job.

But he shouldn't have been out in the field with these men.
He would spit blood into a drop cloth and wipe the blood
with his hand. Mom was right: he hadn't recovered from the
beating, and he never would. He was a doomed general, signal-
ing his own destruction with a baton.

"House painter," mom told him, "you ought to be in bed."

"Never. Nobody's gonna cage me. I couldn't breathe without the smell of paint."

"Darling, tell that to your lungs."

Chick turned to me. "Baby, I have to surround a hospital
with two hundred men, plan a siege, and spit blood, before your
mother calls me darling."

"Stop it," mom said. "You'll give my son the wrong idea."

Chick didn't even have the luxury of returning to Cedars
of Lebanon for a little holiday. Meyer Lansky had an argument

with his own lieutenant, and Chick fell outside the protective umbrella of the Little Man. Rival contractors sabotaged Chick's "shock treatment." They hired goons to smash the hands of Uncle Chick's best house painters. And they promised to turn Chick into a snowman, to wash him in white paint, and set the paint on fire. The goons threatened his children, strolled into Marsha's classroom at William Howard Taft, rubbed her face in chalk dust, wrote "CHICK EISENSTADT IS A DEAD DUCK" on the blackboard, distributed bubble gum and candy to the students, and disappeared.

Chick hired Russian gangsters to fight the goons, but he had to disband his army of house painters. The tax man had come after him, claimed that he'd been pocketing cash without declaring it as income, that he owed a hundred thousand dollars to Uncle Sam. Chickie couldn't fight goons and the Internal Revenue Service. He went into hiding, wore a false beard.

"Faigele, it's Roosevelt's fault. I have enemies in high places."

"The President doesn't persecute house painters, only dentists who helped elect him. He feeds them to Tom Dewey. But you had generals and admirals on your side. Didn't you pamper their wives with silk stockings? Couldn't you appeal to them?"

"How? And have them admit that they crawled into bed with the black market? They're trying to clean their slate, wipe me off their calendar. They're my enemies, Faigele."

That's where I chipped in. "Uncle, I'll defend you. I promised Darcy I'd become a lawyer."

"Don't forget. I'll need you, Baby, when I'm back in Sing Sing."

We'd have a meal with Chickie once a month. It was always in the afternoon, when Bitter Eagles closed its doors to strangers, and Chick could pluck off his beard. He'd grown gaunt without the restaurant's Russian cake. He'd have coughing fits and sweeten the tea he drank with his own blood.

"Chickie, sign yourself into a hospital, please, or it will be too late."

"I can't surface. Roosevelt will arrest me."

"Idiot. Roosevelt doesn't know you're alive."

"The admirals put me on the President's blacklist."

"What blacklist?"

"People who could be a danger after the war."

"You a danger? My poor Chick. The President has closed his eyes to the Bronx. He's lent us to Dewey."

"Lent us to Dewey," Chick said, and it was the last we heard of him. There were no more rendezvous at Bitter Eagles, no more monthly meals. He was a renegade without luck. And we were the losers. We had to mourn a live man, but mom wasn't always sure that Chick was alive.

"Faigele," I said, "all we have to do is search the cemetery. Chick couldn't stand to be buried outside the Bronx."

"And if he died alone, with that ridiculous beard? The cops will throw him into an unmarked grave."

"The cops aren't that dumb. The beard will fall off, and they'll know it was Chick."

"My little Sherlock Holmes," mom said. "The case is closed."

But it wasn't closed. Because those two black marketeers—Darcy and Chick—haunted Faigele, dead or alive. Mom's mind was like my funny bone. It started playing tricks. She'd stand frozen in her mirror, one eye full of mascara, the other eye dark and bald, and mom was Jekyll *and* Hyde at the same moment. And she'd mutter, "Baby, let's go live with the dentist."

I'd have to reason with her, a boy close to seven, in a Brownie cap, with the remnants of ringworm on his scalp, cold little scars. "Mom, I miss Darcy too, but we can't live with him. He's under the ground. And even if I brought a shovel to Woodlawn and dug up Darcy's coffin, we'd never get in. We'd have to keep the lid open, and the birds would eat our eyes."

"Then we'll live with the house painter."

"We can't find him, Faigele. But I'll leave a message on the wall at Bitter Eagles."

"No messages," mom said. "Roosevelt will arrest him."

"Mom, the President can't bother with Chick. He's running against Dewey."

"Then we'll ask Dewey to find him."

"Dewey's a gangbuster. He'd really arrest Chick."

Boss Flynn summoned Faigele to the Concourse Plaza. She didn't want to go, but I persuaded her. "Mom, he's boss of the Bronx and Manhattan and the whole country. He might have some news about Chick."

I had to prepare Faigele's bald eye. I marched her to the Concourse Plaza. Flynn was in the mezzanine, where he'd set up his own headquarters for Roosevelt's reelection campaign. Mr. Lions was with him, but Flynn did the talking, and Lions served the coffee.

"We'll need a woman of character," he said. "Our own Madame Curie. Otherwise the office will be drab. And Mr. Frank has given us his word that he'll drive through the Bronx on one of his whirlwind tours. I wish I could invite you to sit with us in his limousine, but there won't be enough room . . . Fannie dear, wouldn't you like to shake the President's hand at party headquarters?"

"Only if I can ask him about Mr. Dewey and the dentist."

The big fat giant squinted at our borough president. "Mr. Lions, you assured me that Faigele was a sensible girl . . . Here I offer her a presidential handshake, and I get kicked like a dog."

"God forbid. Boss, she didn't mean it . . . Faigele, tell him you're sorry. Mr. Flynn has a kind heart. He's giving you a plum. He's willing to make you manager of the Bronx County Democrats."

"Mr. Lions," mom said, "I'm a card dealer. I don't count coffee cups."

Flynn clutched his suspenders. "The next thing she'll tell me is that she's voting for Tom Dewey."

"No," said the dark lady. "I'm not voting at all."

"That's sacrilege. A Democrat who doesn't vote is a friend of the devil. I promised Mr. Frank that every single registered Democrat in the Bronx would vote for him."

"Mr. Flynn," mom said, "you should have asked me before you made that promise."

"Fannie dear, we own the Bronx. We can lend you glory . . . or toss you out of our camp."

"I only went to night school, Mr. Flynn, but even I know that glory can't be lent."

"Your husband was once an air-raid warden. I can reinstate him, get him a captaincy."

"I still wouldn't vote."

"Boss," Mr. Lions said. "She's beside herself, grieving for the dentist."

"And she blames me. Darcy was a good soldier. He did what he had to do. He was a pauper when I found him, didn't have a dime. I commanded every Democrat under my wing to use Darcy as their dentist . . . and if you persist in your foolishness, you will be a most unfortunate woman, with a family of out-casts on a Democratic island."

"The Bronx is not an island, Mr. Flynn; you only think it is."

And that was the end of the meeting. We never got close to the Democrats again. I liked Mr. Lions, and I liked the Concourse Plaza. But I didn't like them enough to trample on my memory of the dentist. I even bought a Dewey button from a crippled girl in the street, and I was spiteful enough to wear it, but I had to admit that Dewey was no bargain. The dentist would still have his card game and that wonderful chair if Dewey hadn't picked on him . . .

Roosevelt kept his word. He did come to the Bronx, and he rode with Mr. Flynn. The Sea Scouts marched in front of Flynn, like in the last parade, and the Rathcarts were with

them. But Harvey wasn't there. He wouldn't leave Arizona
to wiggle around in white spats and march in another parade
with the Rathcarts. I hid the Dewey pin inside my shirt.

The President was bundled in a big coat. He wore his election hat, an old gray fedora. It felt like every Democrat in cre-
ation had traveled up to the Concourse to catch a glimpse of
FDR. He was still our god, a god who'd turned on the Paley
Charyns. Dad couldn't keep from crying. "Our commander
in chief."

That old gray fox with the twisted legs, who'd contracted
a child's disease when he was a grown man, who couldn't walk
a step without a pair of metal sticks, but had to carry a whole
war on his shoulders, under his Navy cape. Hitler called him
the man with no legs. Hitler was a liar. FDR could play water
polo and swim like a sea lion, and he could have broken Hitler's
back in the water. He was only helpless on land. And maybe
I was conceited, a snot-nosed kid, but I likened his polio to
ringworm. We'd both caught a crazy disease. I'd recovered,
but weren't we cousins under the skin? I loved FDR. We all
did. He was elected before I was born, and no one, not even
George Washington, who'd fought one of his biggest battles on
Harlem Heights, just across from Yankee Stadium, had served
as long as FDR. It was party politics that kept us apart. The
Democrats were making war on mom, and I couldn't aban-
don her, even if FDR and I had both been through the fire
of a child's disease. Polio was worse than ringworm, but at least
the sores on my head had given me the imagination to deal
with Mr. Frank's twisted legs.

Faigele couldn't even buy on credit at the grocery store:
that's how far the Democrats' fat little fingers could reach.
Mom had been wrong. The Bronx was a Democratic island.
Dad thought of moving to Far Rockaway. We'd have the beach
and the boardwalk; and I would have been much closer to the
sharks and submarines in the Atlantic, even Herman Melville's

white whale. Whales could live two hundred years, according
to the Bronx almanac. But Faigele wasn't interested in white
whales, and she wasn't going to let Boss Flynn drive us out of
the Bronx.

Dad convinced her to leave the Concourse, a boulevard
that could only remind her of Darcy and Bitter Eagles. And
we returned to the East Bronx, where we'd lived until I was
four and a half. It was like a huge bandanna of crooked streets
on a relentless checkered plain. Boss Flynn hardly went there.
He had one little storefront that he opened a month before
national elections and closed immediately after. It would have
given him a bad image to register people who wouldn't vote.
The dentist had gone into the East Bronx once to break the
heads of these nonvoters, and he'd come back utterly com-
promised; the more heads he broke, the fewer voters there
were in the East Bronx.

Now we didn't have to worry about Flynn's fat fingers. We
had a bigger apartment, because the rents were cheaper in the
East. I had my own bed, and a little radio, and I could listen
to "Lux Presents Hollywood," a condensed version of current
Hollywood hits with lesser stars in the main roles . . . Tom Neal
in *Casablanca* and Barbara Britton in *Madame Curie*. And slowly,
slowly, the Concourse became a forgotten landscape, a lost article on a growing boy's map.

I missed one thing: nobody in the East called mom
"Madame Curie." But who could I blame? There were no dentists like Darcy floating around, no house painters like Chick,
not even a holy terror like Marsha Eisenstadt. Some kind of
raw intelligence and electric wit seemed to have gone out of
the world. But I had my radio. And I was studying lists of
words, writing rude sentences, while I dreamt of that lawyer I
would become for Darcy's sake, defending political prisoners
and other victims of Republican and Democratic misjustice.
Barrister Baby Charyn.

Wyatt Earp

The East had its Titans, like the West. But they weren't politicians or dentists who broke a lot of heads. Politics didn't count this far from the Concourse. There wasn't even a proper temple where I could have taken art classes. We lived in a kind of isolated anarchy, and within this anarchy was a black man, Haines, the superintendent of our building. Everybody called him Super. He must have been fifty-five, but he looked younger than my own dad. He'd been a foot soldier in the First World War, part of a black regiment that was funneled into the French Army and fought in the Argonne forest. He had battle scars all over his body. He stayed in France after the war, wearing the uniform of a soldier in a French division, and when his uniform began to rot, he returned to the Bronx. Haines had a wife, a girlfriend, four children, and one grandchild, all of whom lived with him in the basement. The Super was a bit like Bat Masterson and Wyatt Earp. He kept the peace in a neighborhood that wasn't known for lawfulness.

Haines wasn't part of any protection racket. He wouldn't charge a shopkeeper whenever he ran in to flatten a drunk who was on the rampage. And any gang that stole goods from one of Haines' stores soon learned to give back the goods or lose its "license" to walk the streets. Haines was a better gangbuster than Tom Dewey. He'd storm a gang's headquarters and demolish the furniture and the chiefs. And if the Irish or Italian fathers of a gang went into the basement looking for the Super, they'd always come out wiser and humbler men. Haines would battle them six at a time, banging heads, biting ears; if one of these dads dared arrive with a gun, Haines would pluck it out of his hand, smash the barrel against a wall, and oblige this dad to eat his own gun.

The cops had little presence in the East, and the shopkeepers of Southern Boulevard and Boston Road understood where the wind blew in the Bronx; their safety could only lie with the battler, Haines. He wouldn't accept money from them, he wouldn't accept bribes, but he couldn't stop them from offering trinkets to his family. The battler was a poor man, but at least his granddaughter had a crib, and his women and children were warm in the winter. That's the only edge he would tolerate. He reminded me of the rat man, Launcelot Perry, who adored dark places and would never have beaten up people for personal profit.

He was also kind to Faigele and her boy with the Brownie cap on his brains. He liked to think of Faigele and himself as foreigners—Europeans, he said. Exiles. But he wasn't European. He was born in the Bronx. He'd had a whole other family in France, a wife and a child he had to leave behind because the gendarmes had come after him (he stole to keep alive). Haines mixed me up with his lost son. I'd go into the basement with him after school and help him shovel coal into the furnace. His face always had a beautiful light against the burning coals. He'd shovel without a shirt, and I could see his war wounds, scars that ran like irregular fingers under the skin. He wouldn't call me Baby. He said I was too old to have a nickname like that.

"Super, have a heart. I'm only seven."

"But I'm not gonna address you like an infant. You have a name. Jerome."

"That's for school," I said. "I'm Baby to mom and dad and my brother, Harvey, and my friends."

"How many friends you got, Mr. Jerome?"

"One at the moment. You."

"Well, that proves my point. And it's a sad commentary if your only friend is a grandpa and a cripple."

"Wish I was your kind of cripple. You're the battler. Our Wyatt Earp."

Haines started to laugh. "That's considerate. Comparing me to a homicidal thief."

"Super, what does *homicidal* mean?"

"Am I your teacher, Mr. Jerome? . . . *Homicidal* means born to kill."

"But Wyatt Earp was a lawman. In Arizona. Where my brother lives."

"Ain't that a coincidence. Well, I met that man when I was a porter at the big station in Los Angeles. I had to carry him off the train, he was so drunk, pissing all over his pants."

"Wyatt Earp?"

"Earpy is what he called himself. He wouldn't go into the toilet alone. Said he'd give me a dollar if I'd help him. His hands were too unsteady to unbutton his fly. Told him I couldn't take a dollar from Wyatt Earp, and it wouldn't be decent if people caught him in the white man's toilet in his condition. Earpy agreed. I took him into the porter's toilet and cleaned him up. And that's when he volunteered his story about the gunfighting business. He wasn't no sheriff in Arizona. He was an armed guard and a detective for Wells, Fargo."

"Who's Wells, Fargo?"

"What they learning you at school? Wells, Fargo was the biggest company in the world for carrying silver and gold. And it seems that Wyatt carried off some of that silver and killed a couple of people."

"Super, I know you wouldn't lie, but I can't believe it."

"Well, history speaks for itself. Just look up Wyatt Earp in the cyclopedia. You can read, can't you, Mr. Jerome? What you gonna be when you grow up?"

"A lawyer," I said.

The Super laughed again. "You mean a crook with the privilege of cheating people?"

"I wouldn't cheat. I'd protect you if you ever had to go and sit in the Tombs."

"Baby, I've been to the Tombs. And the only thing I didn't need was a lawyer."

"I'm not Baby," I said. "I'm Jerome."

And I ran out of the basement with coal dust in my hair . . .

The economy was booming, but dad sat home more and more, saddled with illnesses he'd invent for himself, and mom found a job in a candy factory. She would spend hours dipping cherries into a barrel of chocolate. The factory was in a rotten neighborhood on Edgewater Road, filled with rats who traveled from warehouse to warehouse, and Haines volunteered to walk mom home whenever she had to work late.

Sometimes he brought me along, and I'd marvel how other men would instinctively inch away from him. Haines wasn't very tall. But he had the dancing step of an acrobat and the dark eyes of Wyatt Earp, as I imagined them in my own head. And once, when three men raced out from behind the wall of a warehouse and tried to grab Faigele's purse (with her pay envelope inside), I watched the Super go into gear. He only had to pivot once. His arms lashed out as he turned to protect Faigele and sock the three men in the throat. They bumped into each other without the purse, which was already back under Faigele's arm.

But mom had to pay a price for Haines' gallantry. His girlfriend, Nita, was very jealous. She was a mulatto who looked like Lena Home, the most beautiful woman in America. Nita was the wild lady of the building. Haines' wife, Mattie, had a weak heart and never left the basement, but Nita would patrol the stairs, pretending to sweep or mop, and she'd grab at the heels of some boy in the building, pin him against the banister rail if she could, and blow hot breath into his ear. I was her special target.

"You tell your mama to leave my man alone."

Nita was carrying a child in her belly, Haines' child, and she was proud of it. Half the neighborhood was in love with Nita Brown, and the other half called her a rattlesnake who could lick the blood out of a man. I was only a little pisser with scars on his scalp, but if I had a garden somewhere, Nita Brown was the only rattlesnake I'd want.

"Nita," I told her, "mom's not Mata Hari. She didn't flirt with the Super. She didn't even hold his hand. I'm a witness. I was there. He walked her home from the factory, and he was right. Three gangsters tried to steal her paycheck."

"Gangsters?" Nita muttered, tossing back her hair. "Were they niggers or ofays?"

"What's an ofay?"

"Any man with a white dick."

"They were ofays, far as I could tell."

"Then he must have planted them . . . he's always using ofays to help him impress a new piece of tail."

"Mom doesn't have a tail," I told her.

"Come here, Baby," she said, and Nita scooped me into her arms. I sat above her belly, could see the tiny golden hairs of her mustache, sniff the perfumed well between her breasts.

"Can you hear him knocking?"

"Who's knocking?"

"My little boy . . . Dynamite. That's what I'm gonna call him."

I had my drink of paradise, and it was in the East Bronx. But it ended too soon. Nita put me down. Her arms had the same golden hairs.

"Maybe I can be your Mata Hari," she said, and she sashayed toward the basement in a blue housecoat, her belly heaving. And I floated around with Nita's perfumed sweat in my nostrils. I didn't care one little titty about school. The kids in my class were so backward, they'd never been to the Concourse, and they'd never had art lessons either. I was the class whiz, who could talk about Bronx politics like no other boy. "The Bronx reelected Roosevelt," I said (FDR was just beginning his fourth term in the White House). "Boss Flynn and Mr. Lions managed his campaign from the Concourse Plaza. They demolished Mr. Dewey. It was a Bronx massacre."

I was swaggering here and there, dreaming of Nita Brown, when I noticed that the pretzel vendor outside school was damn suspicious. He picked his teeth with a golden toothpick, like the gangsters of Bitter Eagles, wore a herringbone suit that was strictly Feuerman & Marx, and had faint white spots on his shoes.

"How are you, Ringworm?" he said, to throw me off my guard. He'd trimmed his false beard, and he looked like the prince of pretzel vendors.

"Uncle Chick, you didn't have to hurt mom. Couldn't you have written her a postcard telling us you were alive?"

"Postcards can leave a print."

"And don't call me Ringworm. It's unkind."

"I had to attract your attention. Your head was in the clouds."

"What are you doing in the East Bronx?"

"I'm a refugee, the same as you and Faigele."

"A refugee pretzel vendor?"

"It's a good disguise. A million gorillas are after me, including Meyer. Somebody whispered in the Little Man's ear that I stole from him and his people when I was a boss painter."

"Did you steal?"

"From Lansky? Never . . . Ah, it's nice to see you, Baby. Will you give Faigele a kiss?"

I told mom about the new pretzel man on the block, thinking she'd scorn Chick and wouldn't even want to see him for old time's sake. But the dark lady was unpredictable. If Chick had risen in the East, had become a racketeer or a union rep, mom would have avoided him. But a pretzel man appealed to

Faigele.

I was the one who set the rendezvous, because it might not have looked correct for a married woman to meet with a strange pretzel vendor under the eyes of Boston Road shopkeepers. I picked the public library, which was in a colored neighborhood where the shopkeepers would never go. Uncle Chick arrived with his pretzel basket and a red rose. It didn't matter what he'd done, he was mom's cavalier. And when he saw the dark lady, he began to cry.

"Fool," mom said, "it's a public library." But she took this ex-house painter in her arms, rocked him for a minute, and let him go.

"I'm guilty," he said. "Faigele, I became a pretzel man because of you."

"Imbecile," mom said, "it sounds like a sentimental story."

"But it's true. I hired some gorilla to search for all the Faigeles in the East Bronx, and then I did a little scouting on my own and got a license to sell pretzels outside Baby's school. I figured Baby would find me."

"Why didn't you knock on my door?"

"I can't take risks. I'm a wanted man."

The librarian started looking at him, and Uncle Chick brought us and his pretzel basket into the street. We sat in a colored ice cream parlor and had chocolate milk shakes. Mom, Chick, and me must have been born under the same moon, because we were all crazy about anything chocolate.

Chick didn't have an address. He ran from room to room, shaking off Meyer Lansky's people. His only fixture in the world was his pretzel basket. But he couldn't forget about his skills as an entrepreneur. He began to organize the other pretzel vendors so they would have a bit of muscle and could force the suppliers to bring down the price of each pretzel. He had to use an alias, Michael Strogoff, which is the name of some Siberian prince. But the suppliers weren't too happy about this

Michael Strogoff. They hired a local gang, the Pistoleeros, to knock the hell out of Uncle Chick. They hadn't counted on Haines . . .

The battler showed up while the Pistoleeros were preparing to demolish Chick and his pretzel basket. They swallowed all the pretzels and stripped off Uncle's clothes. Michael Strogoff was caught naked in the middle of his own Siberia: winter in the East Bronx. Haines didn't know anything about a pretzel man's problems. He was patrolling the neighborhood, that's all, keeping the peace. He waded into the Pistoleeros with his hands and feet, kicking, punching faces, stifling the gang's war cries, until he could extricate Chick and the basket. The Pistoleeros surrendered and offered to pay for the pretzels they'd eaten.

"You're grounded," Haines told the gang. "Get off the street."

The battler hardly said a word to Chick, didn't even ask him his name. He helped Michael Strogoff into his clothes, and when mom's Siberian prince took out his wallet to reward the battler, the battler said no.

"If my fiancée ever passes by, give her one of your pretzels . . . not a soft one that's been lying out in the weather, but one that you keep under your napkin."

"But how will I be able to recognize your fiancée?"

"Oh, you can't miss Nita. And she won't be shy about introducing herself."

That should have been the end of the tale, but it wasn't. The Pistoleeros' dads started to brood. What irked them most was that the battler had obliged their sons to give money to an unknown pretzel man. They talked to the suppliers, who talked to some union rep, who was affiliated with one of Meyer Lanky's death squads, and that death squad talked to the Little Man himself. It had nothing to do with pretzels or Pistoleeros. The death squad had discovered who Michael Strogoff was. And it bothered the Little Man that a colored superintendent who liked to play sheriff had rescued somebody on Meyer's own shit list.

This death squad—two Polish bakers from Tinton Avenue in the East Bronx—crept into the basement at three in the morning with guns, knives, and baseball bats and got the Super out of bed, told him he could die peacefully or put up a fuss and watch his women and children suffer. Haines laughed like a jackal. "You'll kill them all, no matter what I do." They stabbed the Super, shot him twice, socked him on the head, but he didn't even go down on one knee. He leapt on the bakers, bit off their noses . . .

The battler and his kin were the only ones who walked out of the basement alive. The cops showed up, sifted for clues. Their single curiosity about the case was that a colored superintendent had survived his own gangland execution. They covered the bakers with a filthy blanket and called an ambulance for Haines.

The Super was never the same. He returned from the hospital with a metal plate in his skull. He had to count on his fingers and couldn't even spell his own name. But he was still the only friend I had. He forgot how to shovel coal, and no matter what I did, I couldn't teach him to hold a shovel in his hands. He'd bury himself in the coal bin and stare at the wall.

"Come on, Super. You're still our Wyatt Earp."

"Yeah," he said. "I'm good for sucking peppermints and pissing in my pants. Just like Earpy."

Nita had a miscarriage. It was mom who attended to her, put wet towels on her head, covered her with all the blankets she could find. "Mrs. Fannie," Nita said in her delirium, "can't me and the Super go and live with the angels?"

"No angels," mom said. "Not right now."

Mom was terribly sullen; she couldn't puzzle out why two bakers from Tinton Avenue would want to kill Haines. Chickie had to enlighten us. He was no longer Michael Strogoff. He'd given his pretzel basket away. We met in the library, and he told us who was behind the bakers. Lansky, the Little Man.

"And you couldn't have warned the Super?" Mom was crying now.

"Faigele, it was a *fait accompli.*"

I didn't even have to ask what a *fait accompli* was. Something that couldn't be stopped, like the fingers of fate.

Mom reached across the library table to slap Uncle Chick. It was the saddest slap I'd ever seen. "That's my *fait accompli,* darling . . . the Super saved your life. You owed him yours."

"Faigele, I couldn't . . . I was too scared. And I wasn't sure where or how the Little Man would strike."

Mom grabbed my hand and we left Uncle Chick in the library She had to bear her own responsibility for what had happened to the Super. Chickie's love for her had made him surface in the East Bronx as a pretzel man. And Haines had been reduced to being a little boy again on account of those pretzels.

"You can call me Baby, Mr. Jerome."

But I couldn't. He wasn't Baby to me. He was a wounded warrior.

Roosevelt died while Haines was still in the hospital. He'd had a cerebral hemorrhage at the Little White House in Warm Springs, Georgia. I can't talk about America, but I know how the East Bronx mourned him. The neighborhood seemed to run on slow motion. You couldn't find a trolley car in the street. The shops were empty. Flags suddenly appeared in the windows, and pictures of FDR in his cape. And mom was bedeviled, because she loved Roosevelt and hated Roosevelt for deserting the dentist, giving him to Dewey.

"Baby, I didn't vote for FDR . . . I threw an evil spell on the President."

"Mom, mom, millions of people didn't vote for Roosevelt."

"Not in the Bronx," mom said. "I was the only one. Baby, I loved him so much, the devil took advantage and turned my hate into a big evil bolt that attacked the President's brain."

I'd never be a lawyer. I couldn't prove that mom hadn't killed FDR. She stayed in bed for two weeks and then she went back to the candy factory. Her boss didn't reprimand her. Mom was the best cherry dipper in town. And besides, lots of women were absent without leave after Roosevelt's death. But Faigele couldn't afford to be sick. She was helping Nita Brown.

Nita had to become the new superintendent of our building, or Haines would have lost the basement apartment, and Mattie and the children would have been out on the street. She wasn't strong enough to attend a whole building by herself; mom and the children would sweep the halls and I would run the dumbwaiter after school. I liked being a superintendent's assistant. But we had to cover up for Nita. She was much wilder after the Super lost some of his brains. She would shovel coal without her clothes on. I didn't mind, but tenants began to complain. She was slovenly, they said. A temptress. She would sit on the stairs and fondle her own breasts.

The landlord fired her, gave her a week to vacate with the battler and his brood. Faigele put on her silver fox coat and her best perfume, painted her mouth, and we went to visit the landlord, Harry Harkins, at his office on West Farms Road. Mom didn't have the heart to leave Haines behind in the coal bin, but we couldn't bring him along. It would only have given the landlord ammunition against us.

Harkins owned and managed a hundred and fifty firetraps in the East. We had to wait an hour to see Harry, but when we entered his office, he couldn't stop gazing at mom. He was a man of seventy, with sad, watery eyes. We introduced ourselves, and Harkins kissed my mother's hand.

"Faigele, I'll give you a diamond . . . send the boy away."

Mom tapped him gently on the cheek. "Shame on you, Harry. I'd like you to rehire Nita Brown."

"Haines' witch? Impossible. She has no legal right to be in

the building. She's a squatter."

Nothing could persuade Harry Harkins, not my mother's smile or perfume and war paint. We ran from West Farms Road and got on a bus to the Concourse. It was my only visit in the months we'd been away. The Germans had just surrendered, and the Concourse was in a festive mood. There were banners and electric candles all over Temple Adath Israel. Now no one had to worry that Hitler would ever have lunch in the Bronx.

The buildings basked in a silver light that was peculiar to the Concourse, as if sun and moon had met somewhere in the sky and were shining down on the West Bronx. But mom was in a hurry, and we couldn't pause to remember our past. We galloped into the Concourse Plaza, and found Fred R. Lions holding court in the lobby on his crimson chair. He observed Faigele with a politician's gray eyes.

"Will you go away, woman? You're an outcast, you and that boy with ringworm."

"I told you once. Baby's head has healed."

"But he's still wearing that cursed cap of the St. Louis Browns . . . go away."

"You're my president," mom told him. "I have the right to see you."

"God forbid. You're not a Democrat. You've been drummed out of the corps. I'd lose my seat at the Plaza if the Boss had an inkling you were here . . . Faigele, we're orphans now that Mr. Franklin is gone."

"I need a favor."

"Absolutely not."

"Call Harry Harkins and tell him that Nita Brown is precious to you."

"Who's Nita Brown?"

"A superintendent on Seabury Place."

"She belongs to Wyatt Earp," I said.

Mr. Lions winked at us. "I get it. The sheriff who almost

put Meyer Lansky out of business. I'd like to meet him. But why should I meddle? What's in it for me? . . . Man alive, I missed you. What a crowd we could pull in if you agreed to deal cards for the Democratic Party."

"I will, Fred. One time only. But call Harkins first . . . *Nita Brown.*"

The borough president's eyes lit with the silver color of the Concourse. He had the bellhop bring him a telephone. He pulled Harkin's number out of a little book, dialed, whispered into the phone, returned it to the bellhop, and winked at my mother. "It's done. Your Nita Brown will never be touched . . . Now will you deal for us, Faigele dear?"

Mr. Lions assembled as many Democrats as he could; they sat around a long table while Faigele dealt for them with a Philip Morris in her mouth. I heard mom sing out the same old rigamarole. "Pair of kings . . . possible flush."

The Democrats were enthralled. They left enormous tips for the dark lady. Mom made more money in two hours than she would have made in a week of cherry-dipping. But she'd dealt for Nita Brown, not the money.

Even when she was in the black market, mom had never bothered much with money. The dentist might have broken heads for a living, but in mom's eyes he was an educated man, an idealist who preferred to dream of Chekhov and the boulevard du Tzarewitch rather than mundane matters of the Bronx. I'm not so sure. It wasn't Chekhov that killed him. It was the Democratic Party . . .

We walked away from Mr. Lions, who followed us down the carpeted stairs of the lobby with all the panache of a Bronx president.

"Faigele, I know about your factory. We've had you watched. One day you'll fall into the chocolate barrel, and no one will ever find you."

"Fat chance, Mr. Lions. I survived the tzar, I'll survive a candy factory in the Bronx."

We didn't return to the East right away. Mom had to rock herself out of that poker deck, like any good dealer. She puffed on her Philip Morris, caught that Concourse light, the dark lady from Belorusse, who lived near chocolate cherries, while dad was hounded by demons. He'd never recovered from his lost status as an air-raid warden. Sam had been happiest wearing his white helmet, barking orders during a blackout. He'd stopped visiting whores in Miami. He was no longer the foreman of a fur shop. He had no shop, and he couldn't enter the equation that existed between mom and me.

I was the protected one, Faigele's Anton Chekhov, who still couldn't write a sentence. But I had my own boulevard du Tzarewitch, my own dark lady with a little dog. This dark lady never drowned in Nice, and her little dog named Dog could have been called Jerome. Dog discovered the world through his own mistress . . . and big, strapping men, who looked at the dark lady while Dog looked at them and could "read" the rapture on their faces. The dark lady belonged to Dog, and mom belonged to Baby, not to the firemen and postmen and the cantors of Belorusse or the Bronx. Their gaze could only empower Faigele and me.

We still didn't return to the East. Mom bought a wire shopping cart with her bounty from Mr. Lions' game. I wondered if she was going to scavenge in the street, search for bric-a-brac that people of the Concourse had left out for the garbagemen. But it wasn't junk that mom was after. It was her old market route. While we lived close to the Concourse, Faigele loved to shop at the Italian market on Arthur Avenue, where she could find exotic, long-nosed vegetables and purple olives and eggs with two yolks.

It was a long trip to Arthur Avenue, and I had to wheel Faigele's cart down the hill, past Claremont Park, to Webster Avenue, a kid in a Brownie cap accompanying his mother

who looked like a movie star. I won't remark on all the men
who were struck dumb staring at Faigele. We were on a mission,
and mom never answered their gaze. We took Third Avenue
to Quarry Road and walked around the Catholic hospital for
chronic diseases, *into* Arthur Avenue. I thought I was going
crazy, because it didn't feel like spring or summer. The shopkeepers must have ordered a second Christmas for V-E Day.
Christmas lights were strung across Arthur Avenue in huge
wire crowns with colored bulbs caught within the filigree.
Santa Claus stared at us from the windows.

It was after lunchtime, and Dominick's was closed, but
when a dark lady peered into the restaurant, the countermen
couldn't resist: they reopened Dominick's for us. We had noo-
dles with "angry Arab sauce" *(arrabbiata),* and mom drank dark
red wine. The countermen wouldn't let her pay. "Signorina, it
would insult our honor," they said.

I had to navigate for mom, guide her out of the restaurant,
her head full of red wine. Faigele began to totter in her silver fox
coat, and I was holding her and trying to trundle the cart. We
were about to enter the indoor market when a tattered little
band approached us, men in funny uniforms, with gray mus-
taches and huge, searching eyes. They were Italian prisoners of
war in the company of military policemen with whistles and
helmets and guns. There was something silly about policemen
who looked like animal trainers. It wasn't their fault. They'd
been thrown into a comic situation. Italy had surrendered
ages ago, and prisoners of war should have been sent home,
but not while the Germans occupied most of Italy. Now the
Germans themselves were prisoners of war, and Berlin was a
city of rats and rubble, but these same Italian prisoners of war
who weren't really prisoners were caught in a curious limbo of
nonpersons who didn't have a home. A kind provost marshal
who was holding them at a camp somewhere in the "interior"
(it was a military secret) must have decided to send them on

an excursion to a typical Italian neighborhood. At least that's what the countermen at Dominick's had explained to us. Arthur Avenue had elected to use its old Christmas decorations for these "unfortunate souls."

Weren't they wayfarers, like me and mom? Trapped in the riddle of our own century, celebrating Christmas in May, inside a tiny Italian bubble. They weren't like the firemen who ogled mom; they didn't want to possess the dark lady with their eyes. They were seeking comfort outside a prison camp. And did mom feel her own confinement in their funny clothes and circus-animal gait? They didn't whisper, they didn't leer. They looked. And mom wouldn't withhold herself from these prison clowns. She broke her drunken stride to embrace them, take each prisoner of war in her arms, let them nuzzle the silky fur of her coat, while the military policemen stood amazed, like prisoners themselves, removed from her warmth.

The dark lady kissed each prisoner of war between the eyes. And then she grabbed our little cart and led me into the market's lighted cavern, where I could get away from prisoners and policemen and search for miraculous eggs with two yolks.

I thought of the battler living in his coal bin, and wanted to bring home a long-nosed vegetable or a purple olive that could lend him a little intelligence. But Arthur Avenue couldn't cure the Super. He was an idealist, like Darcy, and look what it cost him. He was a child to his own children in a basement he had once ruled. But he still had the aura of Wyatt Earp. He would wait for mom outside the candy factory, walk her home. And who would dare test his ability to fight? We danced along our own crooked line. The battler, mom, and me, and everybody got out of our way.

About the Author

Jerome Charyn is an award-winning American author. With more than 50 published works, Charyn has earned a long-standing reputation as an inventive and prolific chronicler of real and imagined American life.